THE GREAT LINCOLNSHIRE
QUIZ BOOK

Compiled by
Dick Richardson

D1350344

COUNTRY BOOKS

Published by Country Books/Ashridge Press
Courtyard Cottage, Little Longstone, Bakewell, Derbyshire DE45 1NN
Tel: 01629 640670
e-mail: dickrichardson@country-books.co.uk
www.countrybooks.biz

ISBN 978-1-906789-53-4

British Library Cataloguing in Publication Data.
A catalogue record for this book is available from the British Library.

Printed and bound in England by 4edge Ltd, Hockley, Essex

Questions

1   Braceby was once a centre of?
2   Little Bytham is a small village in South Kesteven situated between Corby Glen and?
3   There are two villages named Fenton in the county. One is in West Lindsey and the other?
4   Newton is a hamlet located east of?
5   Tallington railway station was on the Great Northern Railway between Grantham and Peterborough. It is was closed in?
6   Sibsey Trader Mill is a six-storey windmill with six sails and was completed in?
7   Torksey Castle is a manor house burnt in which year of the Civil War?
8   The Roman name for Lincoln was?
9   The Old Manor House (now a hotel), Allington (5 miles south of Grantham), was built in?
10   What is the postal town for Witham on the Hill?
11   Kimes Busses operate a bus service from Dowsby to Bourne on which day of the week?
12   Elizabeth Claypole (2 July 1629 – 6 August 1658) married John Claypole in 1646. She was the second daughter of?
13   What is the STD code for Fiskerton?
14   Holbeach St. Johns is a small village in South Holland located about 4 miles south of Holbeach, and 7 south-east of?
15   Where is Jerusalem?
16   The priory of Nocton Park was founded by Robert Darcy in honour of St. Mary Magdalene, probably during the reign of?
17   Where is the village of Authorpe?
18   RAF Cammeringham (formerly RAF Ingham) was a Royal Air Force base used by RAF Bomber Command between 1940 and 1945 and the Polish Air Force until?
19   Inside Colsterworth Church, tucked away behind the organ and difficult to photograph, is a stone sundial plate cut with a penknife at the age of nine by?

Fancy that!

In case the maze (Julian's Bower) at Alkborough becomes overgrown or otherwise indistinct, its pattern is recorded, in a 19th century stained glass church window, on the floor of the church porch and also on the gravestone of James Goulton Constable, which is in Alkborough cemetery.

3

Fancy that!

In June 2005, a speed camera that had been operating in Anwick for several years was shown in court to have been enforcing the wrong speed limit. The police had claimed that the speed limit was 30 mph, yet the absence of street lighting meant it was actually 60mph. Some 2,600 drivers had been prosecuted.

20 Faldingworth is a village on the A46 near?
21 Spilsby market day is?
22 When were the Jews were expelled en masse from Lincoln?
23 Sutterton won a Best Kept Village award in?
24 Northorpe is a hamlet in the parish of Thurlby, about a mile south of?
25 Swallow village school was built in?
26 Cowbit (pronounced Cubbit by the locals) is a small village to the south of?
27 Alfred the Great was married at Gainsborough in?
28 What is the STD code for Wilsford?
29 Which village sounds like a nagging woman?
30 Maidenwell is located 6 miles south of?
31 The new library opened in Boultham in June?
32 Dry Doddington is surrounded by the River?
33 Hatcliffe is a small picturesque village lying 7·5 miles south-west of?
34 The former RAF Ludford Magna ceased operations in?
35 Lincoln City Football Club was formed in?
36 At Potterhanworth, a bus shelter was erected adjacent to the village green to commemorate?
37 RAF Elsham Wolds closed in?
38 Harpswell is a village in the West Lindsey district 12 miles north of?
39 Thornton Abbey was founded as a priory in 1139 by?
40 North Somercotes is located midway between the towns of Mablethorpe and?
41 Lincoln Racecourse closed in?
42 Appleby is a small village north-east of?
43 When did King Henry III charter a weekly market and an annual sheep fair for Corby Glen?
44 Fillingham Castle or Summer Castle is a large castellated mansion built in 1760 by?
45 What is the STD code for Pinchbeck?
46 Great Corringham and Little Corringham are 2 miles east of Gainsborough and 9 miles south of?

Fancy that!

In 1841 Ashby de la Launde Hall and estate passed to John William King who was also the parson of Ashby. Now squire and parson he took over the stables and stud and set about breeding racehorses. In 1874 his filly 'Apology' won the Triple Crown of the Thousand Guineas, the Oaks and the St Leger. His activities came to the notice of Bishop Wordsworth of Lincoln who demanded his resignation from the church. King resigned a year later and died shortly afterwards.

47 Which Victorian writer declared, "I have always held... that the cathedral of Lincoln is out and out the most precious piece of architecture in the British Isles and roughly speaking worth any two other cathedrals we have."?

48 Bardney Abbey was dissolved in which year?

49 What are the Hoe Hills at Dowsby?

50 Keal Cotes post office closed in?

51 In which year did Carlby replace the wooden village hall with a fine brick structure?

52 Where is the Lincoln City Football Club's homeground?

53 St Mary's church, Walesby, is an Arts and Crafts style church de signed by the Irish architect, Temple Moore. In 2008 the church was shut after?

54 Chapel St. Leonards is a village situated 5 miles to the north of the resort of?

55 Swallow is a small village on the A46 road just north-east of Caistor and around 2 miles south of?

56 Where is the Newport Arch, the remains of a 3rd century Roman gate?

57 Ancaster stone was noted for the fact that?

58 New Waltham is located close to the A16 just south of Grimsby and?

59 Canwick Hall was the seat of the Sibthorp family from the 17th – 20th centuries, with the present structure being erected in?

60 Tom Woods brewery is at?

61 Rippingale railway station was a station serving the villages of Rippingale, Dowsby and Dunsby on the Great Northern Railway Bourne and Sleaford railway. It opened in?

62 In the late 1930s, an uncultivated tract of land 2 miles east of Barkston village, was prepared as a relief landing ground for aircraft operating from nearby?

63 What is the STD code for North Witham?
64 Coleby church was also extensively restored in 1900. It is one of the very few churches in the country to have what on its steeple?
65 Nocton is a village 7 miles south of?
66 *The Lincolnshire Echo* was founded in?
67 The impressive swing bridge known as Keadby Bridge crosses the Trent near Althorpe to connect the Isle of Axholme to Scunthorpe. What is its other name?
68 Eastville is a small hamlet located north of?
69 Construction of the first Lincoln Cathedral began when the see was removed from?
70 At 16 feet, where is the largest church clock in the country with a single hand?
71 Hackthorn is a village situated 7·5 miles north of?
72 Which motor racing circuit is around 2 miles south of Tathwell?
73 Healing is a village near Grimsby between Stallingborough and?
74 What is the STD code for Flixborough?
75 A Methodist chapel was built at Anton's Gowt by the Doughty family in which year?
76 North Rauceby is a small village of around 150 residents situated 4 miles north-west of?
77 Magna Carta was drawn up in 1215, one of the witnesses was Hugh of Wells, Bishop of Lincoln. One of only four surviving originals of the document is preserved in?
78 Barrow Haven is a hamlet and the site of a former ferry crossing to?
79 Dunsby is a small village located?
80 In Tetford churchyard is a headstone to two gypsies, Tyso Boswell and Edward Hearin. How did they die?
81 What was RAF Ingham was renamed in 1944?
82 Flixborough was at the centre of the UK's worst industrial accidents when the Nypro Works chemical plant was devastated by an explosion in what is known as the Flixborough disaster. Twenty eight people died and more than 100 were injured, with around 100 homes in the village itself being destroyed or badly damaged. When was it?

Fancy that!

Beelsby: According to local legend there is a stone in the middle of the a local farm, called 'Molly Briar's Stone'. At midnight, on the 21st of June each year, a ghost of the maiden is seen sitting on the stone milking a white cow.

Fancy that!

Canwick Hall was the seat of the Sibthorp family from the 17th century – 20th century, with the present structure being erected in 1810. Family members included the botanist John Sibthorp and several MPs, most notably the eccentric Colonel Sibthorp. Having already angered Queen Victoria by his vocal opposition to an allowance for her consort Prince Albert of Saxe-Coburg and Gotha, he went on to declare that the Prince's Great Exhibition project would bring the plague to England. The Hall was later home of Arthur Foljambe, 2nd Earl of Liverpool from 1939 to his death there in 1941.

83 Old Somerby is situated three miles east of?

84 During The Anarchy, in 1141 Lincoln was the site of a battle between King Stephen of England and the forces of?

85 King John gave Scotter a confirmation charter and he visited in?

86 A Royal Flying Corps (RFC) aerodrome at Bracebridge Heath originally opened in?

87 Fillingham Lake is one of the sources of the River?

88 Where are Walt Disney's ancestors buried?

89 Asgarby is a small Lincolnshire hamlet on the A17 Boston to Newark road, between Sleaford and?

90 Which river flows through Hemingby?

91 Brauncewell is a hamlet situated between Leadenham and?

92 King Sweyn, father of Canute, died at nearby Thonock Park, Gainsborough, in?

93 Partney churchyard contains a stone commemorating the marriage of the first circumnavigator of Australia, and Ann Chappelle on 17th April 1801. Who was he?

94 The first Lincoln Cathedral, was completed in 1092; it was rebuilt after a fire but was destroyed by an earthquake in?

95 Baston Football Club was formed by Samuel Spry in which year?

96 Winthorpe is a small village about 2 miles north of?

97 Cranwell manor was held by the Thorold family from the 16th century for over three hundred years and was demolished in?

98 What is the STD code for Gedney?

99 The University of Lincoln started life as the University of Lincolnshire and Humberside in?

100 Obthorpe is a hamlet about a mile south of the village of?

101 In which year did Denton hold its first streetmarket?

102 Waddington opened as a Royal Flying Corps flying training station in?

103 Which church is often referred to as the Cathedral of the Marshes?

104 Tothill church of Saint Mary was built of brick on a stone base, and had some 18th century alterations. It was demolished in?

105 Where is the village of Aunby?

106 RAF Hemswell was located just outside the village from 1937 until it closed in?

107 Who was organist at Lincoln Cathedral and an English composer of the Renaissance?

108 Which river passes through the west part of Barkston?

109 Where did The Darkness record *Permission to Land*, the Arctic Monkeys record *Whatever People Say I Am That's What I'm Not*, and the Automatic record *Not Accepted Anywhere*?

110 Ealand is a small village on the Stainforth and Keadby Canal in the Isle of Axholme, near?

111 Withcall railway station opened in 1876. Passenger services ended on 5 November?

112 Where was the 18th century antiquarian William Stukeley was born in 1785?

113 Trusthorpe is a small village 2 miles south of Mablethorpe and 12 miles north of?

114 Which family established a bus service in Atterby in the early part of the 20th century?

115 Burwell parish church, dedicated to Saint Michael, became redundant in?

116 The deserted medieval village of Gainsthorpe is situated near?

117 Leverton is a village around 6 miles east-north-east of?

118 What is the post town for Deeping St. Nicholas?

119 Legsby forms part of the district of West Lindsey and is located 13 miles south of Caistor and 3·5 miles south-east from?

Fancy that!

Poet John Gillespie Magee was killed after a mid-air collision on 30 June 1941 while stationed at RAF Digby with No 412 (Fighter) Squadron, RCAF. Magee is buried in Scopwick. On his grave are inscribed the first and last lines from his poem High Flight:

"Oh! I have slipped the surly bonds of Earth –
Put out my hand and touched the Face of God."

120 What was the name of the Aswardby parish priest (1881-1892) prosecuted and imprisoned for Ritualist practices in 1876 and 1880 (and is thus regarded as something of a martyr by Anglo-Catholics)?

121 Lincoln Central Railway Station was designed in?

122 Fillingham is a village in the West Lindsey district and is 9 miles north of?

123 Reepham shares its village hall with neighbouring?

124 In St Lawrence's Church, Aylesby, the pews were hand crafted in 1759 by James Harrison of Middle Rasen. Who was his famous brother?

125 Goulceby was the birthplace of William Marwood, hangman, who invented?

126 Little Bytham's church is uniquely dedicated to St Medard and St Gildard. Who were they?

127 Just outside Wainfleet All Saints is an old windmill which forms part of the original?

128 In 2009 Kelly Adams joined the cast of long-running BBC1 drama series *Hustle* for its fifth season. She was born 16 October 1979. But where?

129 Ancaster was a Roman town on the junction of King Street with?

130 What is the STD code for Metheringham?

131 Sir Isaac Newton's mother, Hannah Ayscough, and father, also called Isaac, are both buried in which church?

132 Holton cum Beckering is a small village in West Lindsey and lies 6 miles south of?

133 Where is Burghley House, one of the best Elizabethan mansions in the country?

134 West Butterwick is 4 miles north-east of Epworth and 4 miles north of?

135 Holton Village Halt was a railway halt on the East Lincolnshire Railway which served the village of Holton-le-Clay in Lincolnshire between 1905 and?

136 Monksthorpe chapel is in the ownership of?

137 East Stockwith is separated by the River Trent from West Stockwith, Nottinghamshire. The two villages were once connected by a ferry, but this stopped in?

138 Bullington is a village about 8 miles north-east of?

139 Grayingham church is dedicated to Saint Radegund. Who was she?

140 What is the STD code for Chapel St. Leonards?

141 During the Dissolution of the Monasteries how many monasteries within Lincoln closed down?

142 Great Coates railway station was built by the Great Grimsby and Sheffield Junction Railway in?

143 Little Hale is a hamlet directly south of the larger villages of Great Hale and Heckington, 5 miles from the town of?

144 Bernie Taupin, the English lyricist famous for his collaboration with Elton John was born in which village on 22 May 1950?

145 In Donington church is a memorial to Matthew Flinders, who charted the coastline of?

146 New York is a hamlet in East Lindsey district on the B1192 road north of?

147 When did the Lincon Cathedral's great spire rot and collapse?

148 Bishop Oliver Sutton (1280-1299) was responsible for the re-naming of this village, coining the name Ashby Puerorum. What does it mean?

149 Bardney Abbey belonged to which monastic order?

150 Sutterton lies approximately 7 miles south-south-west of?

151 What is the STD code for Barrowby?

152 Morton Hall, near Swinderby is the location of?

153 Cadwell Park, near Louth, was established in 1934 by?

154 The Houblon Inn at Oasby is named after?

155 Leasingham is a village in the District of North Kesteven and is situated less than two miles north of?

Fancy that!

The Haxey Hood is a traditional event in at the village of Haxey in North Lincolnshire, on the afternoon of 6 January, the Twelfth Day of Christmas (though if this falls on a Sunday, it is held on 5 January).

It is a kind of large rugby football scrum (called the "sway"), which pushes a leather tube (called the "hood") to 1 of 4 pubs, where it remains until the following year's game.

The official story is that in the 14th century, Lady de Mowbray, wife of an Isle landowner, John De Mowbray, was out riding towards Westwoodside on the hill that separates it from Haxey. As she went over the hill her silk riding hood was blown away by the wind. Thirteen farm workers in the field rushed to help and chased the hood all over the field. It was finally caught by one of the farm workers, but being too shy to hand it back to the lady, he gave it to one of the others to hand back to her. She thanked the farm worker who had returned the hood and said that he had acted like a Lord, whereas the worker who had actually caught the hood was a Fool. So amused was she by this act of chivalry and the resulting chase, that she donated 13 acres of land on condition that the chase for the hood would be re-enacted each year.

156 St Mark's Church, Amcotts, built 1853-1859, was designed by the Goole architect?

157 What is the Dunston Pillar?

158 Nettleham is located between the A46 and A158, four miles north-east of?

159 What is the STD code for Althorpe?

160 Which RAF base is home to the Battle of Britain Memorial Flight, with a number of historic airplanes making regular flights?

161 Tathwell Church is dedicated to?

162 Leadenham is a village in North Kesteven, bypassed to the south in 1995 by the A17. It is on the A607 between Welbourn and?

163 A plaque to the memory of the American airmen who died when their plane crashed on Wrangle Common is in Wrangle church. What date was it?

164 Barton Waterside consists of the former port area at the north end of?

165 Lincoln City were notably the first club managed by?

166 At 295 feet, which is the tallest parish church spire in England?

167 Metheringham railway station was opened to passengers on?

168 Broxholme is a village about 8 miles north-west of?

169 Scothern parish church is dedicated to?

170 Whitton is a village about 9 miles west of?

171 Nocton and Dunston railway station (GNR/GER Joint) was closed in?

172 Where was Alfred Lord Tennyson's father minister of the church from 1807 to 1831?

173 The Folkingham Gas Light Company was founded in?

174 Close by to the east of the Ingoldsby is the Roman road King Street that ran from Bourne to?

175 North Cockerington is a small village found approximately 4 miles to the east of?

176 An early medieval nunnery founded at Threekingham in the late 7th century by Saint Werburh and dedicated to Saint Æthelthryth, was destroyed by the Danes in?

177 Where was Sir Neville Marriner, English conductor and violinist, born 15 April 1924?

178 Addlethorpe, off the A52 west of Ingoldmells has a golf course of 6,400-yards and has an unusual par of?

179 What was built on the green in the centre of Dyke to mark the millennium?

180 The only remains of a substantial Roman villa or high status Romano-British farmhouse in Lincolnshire are located in a large field at the south end of the village of?

181 Baumber is a village in the East Lindsey district about four miles north of?

182 There are two villages named Frieston in the county. One is in Holland, and the other?

183 Careby village school was opened in 1869, and closed before?

184 Jim Broadbent (born 24 May 1949) is known for his role in *Bridget's Jones' Diary*. He also appears in the Harry Potter films as Horace Slughorn. Where was he born?

185 Eastoft post office closed in?

186 Uffington and Barnack railway station was opened in 1846 and closed to passengers in?

187 Where is Lincolnshire's last surviving post mill?

188 What is the STD code for Billingborough?

189 A Wesleyan Chapel and Sunday school was built in Keal Cotes in?

190 Castle Bytham has an 11th century Norman castle mound; the castle itself was destroyed by Henry III in?

191 Nettleham is located between the A46 and A158, four miles north-east of?

192 Where is Jews' Court, the oldest synagogue in the British Isles?

193 Why is Bigby one of the Thankful Villages in Lincolnshire?

194 Pode Hole is a small village to the west of?

195 What is the village emblem for South Kyme?

196 Where was Sir Isaac Newton born in 1642?

197 On 27 February 2008, the Haconby parish church spire was damaged by?

198 Mareham le Fen is located on the A155 road; the nearest town being?

199 Where did Raengeires, a Briton, defeat the Saxon general Horsa in a great battle?

200 Anton's Gowt: The word Gowt is on old term for?

201 What disaster befell Carlton Scroop church in 1632?

202 The Museum of Lincolnshire Life, Lincoln, occupies a listed former barracks, built in?

203 Edenham is a village situated about three miles north-west of?

204 Carlby had a new village sign erected on the village green at a cost of £3,200 to mark?

Fancy that!

Melton Ross. The de Ros family had a long feud with the Tyrwhit family from the nearby village of Kettleby. According to legend in 1411 the Tyrwhits attacked Melton Ross Manor with 500 men. The disagreements continued, and some 200 years later James I erected gallows at a point close to the village, ordering that any deaths from the feud be treated as murder. The gallows are still standing, between Melton Ross and the nearby village of Wrawby.

Fancy that!

Moulton. All Saints' Church was built in about 1180, instigated by Prior John of Spalding. It took approximately 60 to 70 years to build, and was heavily restored from 1866 to 1867 by William Smith. The church has a particularly wonderful rood screen, dating from around 1425. There is an intriguing headstone in the floor of the church, which is that of Prudence Corby, who apparently died on "July 36 1793". No explanation has been offered for the error.

205 Gunness (or Gunhouse) is a small village situated on the east bank of the River?

206 There are two hamlets called Aisby. Where are they?

207 What is the dialling code for Haxey?

208 Quarrington, Sleaford. Rauceby Mental Hospital, originally called Kesteven County Asylum, closed in?

209 West Ashby is a village a mile north of the market town of?

210 Theddlethorpe is a village Situated approximately 4 miles north of?

211 The first documentary evidence of Julian's Bower (maze) at Alkborough seems to date from writings of the Yorkshire antiquary Abraham de la Pryme in which year?

212 An airfield was established at Elsham Wolds as early as?

213 What is the STD code for Kirkstead?

214 In January 2010 the Aveland school at Billingborough merged with a Sleaford school to form?

215 Heighington Grammar School was founded in 1621 and closed in?

216 The Engine Shed is a music and entertainment venue in Lincoln. When did it open?

217 The parish church at Ashby de la Launde is dedicated to?

218 Canwick is a small village two miles south of?

219 Old Leake is a village around eight miles north-east of?

220 Close to Winceby is the Snipe Dales nature reserve and country park, owned by?

221 Bishop Norton is about 10 miles west of?

222 RAF Faldingworth was used by Bomber Command during World War II and closed in?

223 When did the Methodist chapel at Anton's Gowt close?

224 Carlton Scroop was once split in half by the Honington and Lincoln railway, opened in?

225 Hartsholme Country Park, Lincoln, covers more than 200 acres opened in?

226 Thornton Abbey was dissolved in?

227 Beckingham is by the Nottinghamshire border and the River Witham and on the A17 road east out of?

228 Ewerby is a small village located north-east of Sleaford near?

229 What is the STD code for Firsby?

230 Horbling is a village in South Kesteven situated a half mile north of?

231 South Witham is bisected by the young River?

232 What is the population of Braceby?

233 Ashby by Partney is a small hamlet located south off the A158, east of?

234 Which English Civil War battle was fought between Foston and Marston in 1643?

235 St. Margaret's Church, Langrick, was built in?

236 Panton is a village in the civil parish of East Barkwith, it is 14·4 miles north-east of?

237 The Golden Eagle, Lincoln, is a brick built, cream painted old coaching house built in?

238 Althorpe Primary School opened in which year?

239 Cagthorpe is an area of Horncastle south of and separated from the historic town centre by the re-aligned River?

240 Glentworth Hall is a large Elizabethan country house built by?

241 The Louth Navigation ran from Tetney until?

242 Henry Kirke White, the Nottingham poet to whom are attributed the words of the hymn *Oft in danger, Oft in woe*, was educated at which Rectory in 1804-5?

243 What is the STD code for Bicker?

244 Frognall is a small village lying north east of?

245 Which family established a bus service in Atterby in the early part of the 20th century?

Fancy that!

Nettlestone. On Boxing Day, shoemakers would traditionally "beat the lap-stone" at the house of any "water drinkers" (i.e. teetotaller), to mock them. This refers to a story from the 18th century in which a Nettleton resident called Thomas Stickler, who had stayed off alcohol for twenty years, got tipsy after half a pint of ale at his shoemaker's on Christmas Day. When questioned by his wife, he replied that he was not drunk but had simply fallen "over the lap-stone". Hence, the day after every Christmas, shoemakers would carry out the above practical joke.

246 St James Church at Dry Donningtonand is well known for?

247 Since 1987, Grasby has been twinned with the small French village of?

248 Lincoln Drill Hall was originally constructed as a military and police training hall in which year?

249 Bassingthorpe is a tiny village lying south of Grantham, on C class road between the B6403 to the west and the B1176 to the east. It contains?

250 The Knights Templar had only two infirmaries in England. One was in this county. Where?

251 Firsby railway station was closed in?

252 During the Second World War, Blyton was the home of a bomber airfield – RAF Blyton which was abandoned in which year?

253 East Kirkby is a village situated on the A155 south of?

254 What is the STD code for Hough-on-the-Hill?

255 Cold Hanworth is a village situated 7 miles north-north-east of?

256 Gedney railway station was closed in?

257 There are three Weltons in Lincolnshire: Welton by Lincoln, Welton le Wold and?

258 Aswardby (pronounced as-ard-bee) is a few miles north west of?

259 Sibsey Free Primary School was established in?

260 Where was Jonathan Kerrigan born on 14 October 1972? An English actor well known for his portrayal of gay nurse Sam Colloby in the BBC medical dramas *Casualty* and *Holby City,* and as police officers in the series *Merseybeat* and *Heartbeat.*

261 Belton House is administered by?

262 Haverholme Priory was a monastery situated 4 miles north east of Sleaford near?

263 Creeton is a hamlet located 5 miles south west of?

264 What is the STD code for Gosberton?

265 Spital-in-the-Street is a small hamlet on the Roman Ermine Street (hence the suffix). It forms the modern A15 road, near its junction with the A631 road, known as Caenby Corner, 12 miles north of?

266 Wragby railway station closed to passengers in?
267 The nearest market town for Keal Cotes is?
268 Ancaster was the Roman station of?
269 Bolingbroke Castle was the birthplace of?
270 Sir Isaac Newton was a student at the Grammar School in?
271 Bonby about 5 miles south of?
272 The Plough Inn, Garthorpe closed in?
273 Where is the location of the Radcliffe Donkey Sanctuary?
274 Long Bennington is a village in South Kesteven equidistant from Newark-on-Trent and?
275 North Thoresby is a village in Lincolnshire situated between Louth and?
276 Where was the last working mill in England to grind woad?
277 What is the STD code for Boultham?
278 Great Coates is a village to the north-west of?
279 Ashby Hall at Ashby de la Launde was built in 1595 by?
280 Tumby Woodside railway station opened in 1913 serving the Great Northern Railway, and closed in?
281 Lincoln's Medieval Bishop's Palace is maintained by?
282 Bloxholm lies about a mile south-west of the village of?

Fancy that!

Northorpe. Nanny Rutt. The story begins with a young girl, given different names in versions, who had arranged to meet with a lover at the well in Math wood. The girl sets off into the wood in the early evening, but on her way, meets an old woman wrapped in a shawl that casts a deep shadow on her face in the evening light. A conversation between the old woman and the girl ensues, and she is warned about the dangers of the wood at night, as well as those of eloping without the permission of her parents. Ignoring these warnings, she continues on her way, and finds her way to the source of the well, deep inside the wood, where she had arranged to meet her lover. Here she waits for a long time, and by the time she realises he is not coming it is very dark. Tears from the rejection in her eyes cloud her vision which already poor due to the darkness of the woods, and she soon become hopelessly lost. Eventually, she stumbles upon a clearing in the woods, which holds an overgrown stone building, little bigger than a small shack. In the doorway stands the old woman, her shawl now pulled back to reveal a hideous face lit by the ghostly moonlight. As she turns to run she stumbles and falls. The old woman's shadow falls on her as she advances, freezing her body with a paralysing chill, and her throat goes dry as she tries to scream. The girl is never seen again.

283 Who lives at Bishop's House, Church Lane, Irby-on-Humber?

284 M. R. James (1862–1936) specialtiy was antiquarian ghost stories, one of which was set in a hall between Sleaford and Threekingham. Demolished after WWII, where was it?

285 Great Ponton is a village approximately three miles south of?

286 What is the STD code for Keal Cotes?

287 RAF Binbrook, located at Brookenby, was opened as a Bomber Command station in June of which year?

288 Honington is a village about 5·5 miles north of?

289 Where is Countess Close, a rectangular earthwork measuring approx. 80m x 90m internally?

290 Grayingham is a small village near Kirton in Lindsey, about 9 miles north-east of Gainsborough and 10 miles south of?

291 Keadby was chosen as the destination for the Stainforth and Keadby Canal which was opened in?

292 Stow Minster was partly built under the patronage of Leofric, Lord of Mercia, and his wife?

293 The first ever tanks were invented, designed and built in Lincoln by William Foster & Co. during?

294 Billinghay is twinned with?

295 What is the full name of Gunby in South Kesteven?

296 During the Reformation of the English church, the vicar of Belchford was hanged, drawn and quartered for treason after leading a rebellion against the crown in which year?

297 Deeping St. James lies east of?

298 Heighington is a village located 4 miles south-east of Lincoln. How is it pronounced?

299 There are two pubs on the Keadby canal side – The Barge Inn and?
300 Where is Europe's largest tram museum?
301 Wootton is a small village situated 5 miles south-east of Barton-upon-Humber, 7 miles north-east of Brigg and 3 miles north of?
302 Beckingham was bypassed at a cost of £600,000 in which year?
303 Goxhill railway station was built by the Great Grimsby and Sheffield Junction Railway in?
304 Irnham Hall was the home the Luttrell family 1418. The early 14th century Luttrell Psalter is now kept at?
305 How many listed buildings are in Caistor?
306 It was at Edenham vicarage that the Australian poet and novelist Frederic Manning stayed when he arrived in the country in?
307 Habrough railway station was built by the Great Grimsby and Sheffield Junction Railway in?
308 Where was the birthplace of Thomas Sutton (b. 1532), founder of Charterhouse School and Hospital in London?
309 Manthorpe is situated about 2 miles west of Thurlby and 3 miles south-west along the A6121 from?
310 Kirkstead Abbey was founded in?
311 George Boole (2 November 1815 – 8 December 1864) was the inventor of Boolean logic — the basis of modern digital computer logic — Boole is regarded in hindsight as a founder of the field of computer science. Where was he born?
312 Sausthorpe (also called Saucethorpe) is a village in the valley of the River Lymn. It is situated 3 miles from?
313 Blankney Golf Club was formed in which year?
314 Grimoldby is a village approximately 5 miles east of?
315 A cold war era bunker of the Royal Observer Corps was built at Carlton Scroop in 1965, and abandoned in?
316 Kirkby Underwood is a village in the district of South Kesteven located around 4 miles north of?
317 Where is the only remaining thatched church in Lincolnshire?
318 Haconby primary school closed in?

Fancy that!

The redundant church at Kingerby contains unusual medieval memorials, including those to members of the Disney family, ancestors of film-maker Walt Disney.

319 Kirkby Green is a small village south-east of Lincoln, south-west of Woodhall Spa, and 8 miles north of?

320 Where is the site of the deserted medieval village of Butyate?

321 Marton windmill is owned by?

322 Scamblesby parish church is dedicated to?

323 Withern (also known as Withern with Stain) is a village 6 miles south east of?

324 The deserted medieval village of Ringsthorpe was located just to the west of?

325 Harmston Hall, is a manor house erected in 1710 for?

326 Habrough a small village located 3 miles to the west of Immingham and 2 miles south of?

327 Lea's primary school is called?

328 Where is the finest bird watching location in south west Lincolnshire?

329 Laceby is a village located on the A46 road just outside the western boundary of?

330 Boultham Mere is a nature reserve looked after by the Lincolnshire Wildlife Trust, created in?

331 What is the STD code for Kirton?

332 Twigmoor Hall near Holme, was the home of John Wright before he was executed for his part in?

333 The manor house at Pickworth dates to?

334 Where was Stephen Russell (Steve) Race OBE, British composer, pianist and radio and television presenter, born on 1 April 1921?

335 Where is the Dixons Wood Nature Reserve?

336 Grimsthorpe Castle lies within a 3,000 acre park landscaped by?

337 Langworth is a small village about 7 miles north-east of?

338 Which small holiday resort is known for its family tennis tournament which has been held in the first week of August every year since 1928 (except for 1939-57)?

339 The Elizabethan statesman William Cecil, later Lord Burghley, was born where in Bourne?

340 Twenty had a railway station from 1866 until its closure in?

341 Brant Boughton Church was heavily restored by the Rector, Canon Frederick Heathcote Sutton and the architect George Frederick Bodley between?

342 In 1930 Harmston Hall became part of a new mental health hospital complex, and functioned as the headquarters for the (now distinctly un-politically correctly named) organisation, the 'Lincolnshire Joint Board for Mental Defectives'. The hospital site finally closed down in?

343 Lea is a small village at the junction of the A156 and?

344 Brigg Grammar School was founded in 1669 by?

345 Harlaxton Manor is the home of?

346 Kimes Busses of Folkingham have been serving South Lincolnshire since?

347 Digby is a small village 6 miles north of the town of?

348 RAF Hemswell was called Harpswell airfield when it first opened in?

349 Lenton is sometimes known as?

350 Markby is a village in East Lindsey, situated approximately 4 miles north-east of?

351 All Saints' church Moulton is known as?

352 There was a Grade II listed triple aircraft hangar at Bracebridge Heath of unique interest (a Belfast truss hangar), but this was sadly demolished in?

353 Where is the nearest railway station for Digby?

354 Heydour is a hamlet in the South Kesteven district and is 5 miles southwest of Sleaford and 6 miles north-east of?

Fancy that!

Eric Todd, a boatman on the canal, had much to say on the subject of 'horse-marines'. The custom appears to have been, whoever caught a keel's rope when it was thrown to the jetty was hired, and the 'marines' who stabled their horses by the 'Friendship Inn' in Keadby would tow the keel to its destination. The 'horse-marines' wore distinctive clothing which consisted of a black trilby hat, a muffler, corduroy trousers and waistcoat. They all carried a whip tucked into a massive leather belt.

355 What is the STD code for Edenham?

356 In November 2007, The Red Cow at Quadring was sold off, and has opened up as an Indian restaurant named?

357 Langtoft is a village on the A15 road, about 10 miles north of Peterborough and about 8 miles east of?

358 Braceborough Spa was popular in the Victorian era for its natural spring waters. A bath house was built in?

359 Sedgebrook railway station was closed in?

360 Sir Isaac Newton's birthplace, Woolsthorpe Hall, is administered by?

361 Lincoln Arboretum is a 22 acre park in Lincoln. It was designed and laid out between 1870 and 1872 by the celebrated Victorian gardener?

362 The six bells in St. Mary's Church, Welton, were cast by Henry Harrison. Who was his famous uncle?

363 Which RAF base is near Brattleby?

364 Foston is a small village in the South Kesteven district situated 6 miles north-west of?

365 What is the STD code for Deeping St. Nicholas?

366 Waltham Windmill was originally built in 1666, but was blown down several times. It was last re-built in?

367 Tothill is a village located about 6 miles south-east of Louth, and about 5 miles north-west of?

368 Branston Hall was built between?

369 Heckington Methodist Church was built in 1904 by the architect?

370 Matthew Flinders of Donington was apparently inspired to launch a nautical career after reading?

371 Holbeach Drove is a village in South Lincolnshire at the junction of the B1166 and the B1168. The village church is dedicated to St. Polycarp. Who was he?

372 RAF North Witham opened in 1943 and was used by both the Royal Air Force and United States Army Air Force. It was closed in?

373 Home Defence Flight Station Brattleby (also known as Brattleby Cliff) was opened on the site of the current RAF Scampton in?
374 Helpringham railway station closed in?
375 Quadring is a small village north of Gosberton, Lincolnshire. Humorously the name literally means?
376 Where is the popular Brigsley Home-Made Ice Cream manufactured?
377 The Lincoln Performing Arts Centre (LPAC) is a 446-seat multi-purpose auditorium. When did it open?
378 Where is Julian's Bower, a unicursal turf maze, 43 feet across, of indeterminate age?
379 Fulletby is a village northeast of Horncastle, and northwest of?
380 Lea's nearest railway station is Gainsborough Lea Road on the Sheffield to?
381 St Mary's Church, Walesby, was damaged in the 1930s when its 'candle snuffer' spire was dislodged resulting in its eventual removal. What caused the damage?
382 RAF Hibaldstow was commissioned on 12 May?
383 During his retirement the actor and war hero Richard Todd lived in Little Humby, where he died in?
384 What is the name of the Brookenby theatre?
385 West Halton is 2·5 miles north-west of Winterton, and 7 miles north of?
386 Which author wrote *The Commonwealth of Oceana* (1656)?
387 Cadney cum Howsham is in North Lincolnshire and consists of the small villages of Cadney and Howsham. The parish boundary is defined by water on all sides by the Old River Ancholme, Kettleby Beck and?
388 Mavis Enderby, the unusual name for a tiny hamlet nestling in the rolling hills of the Lincolnshire Wolds, east of?

Fancy that!

Scampton. In the late 1950s, as a preliminary to road widening work by Lincolnshire County Council, the gate guardian – then a Grand Slam bomb – had to be moved. Efforts to lift it with a small crane proved futile, as it was much heavier than expected. Upon closer examination, it was found to be still filled with live explosives. It was carefully removed on an RAF low loader and detonated on a test range. It is unclear how a live bomb managed to be put on display, but it seems that it was in place for well over a decade.

Fancy that!

In 1945 fields adjacent to Caenby were a military Q decoy site maintained by RAF Hemswell. Dummy plywood buildings, inflatable rubber aircraft or vehicles and a ploughed faux runway were set up to simulate an active airfield and draw German bombers away from genuine target airfields.

389 Close to Braceborough is Braceborough Spa, which had its own station. This was on the independent Essendine-Bourne Railway, which became part of the Great Northern Railway. The line was closed in June?

390 Hemswell is a village in the West Lindsey district on the A631 between Caenby Corner and?

391 Denton is an ancient Roman settlement nestling just south west of?

392 Which Lincolnshire village did John Wesley describe as 'an earthly paradise'?

393 The gateway to Coleby Hall is an imitation ruined Roman arch based upon?

394 Hibaldstow is a small village in North Lincolnshire 4 miles south of?

395 What is the STD code for Messingham?

396 RAF Digby was formerly?

397 Fiskerton Church has a picture of the Madonna and Child by 17th century Italian artist, Carlo Dolci. Who gave it to the church?

398 Riseholme Park campus covers more than?

399 Wilsthorpe is a village 4 miles south of?

340 The oak reredos (early 1920's) behind the altar of St John the Baptist's Church, Alkborough, was hand made by the famous? (Clue: The right hand upright has his mouse trademark.)

341 Holme is located some five miles south-east of?

342 What is the Boston Stump?

343 Laceby parish church is dedicated to?

344 Goxhill lies 4·9 miles east of Barton-upon-Humber and 9·7 miles north west of?

345 The hall at Witham on the Hill was once owned by descendents of Archdeacon Robert Johnson. Which famous public schools did he found?

346 Brandon Church was restored in 1872 by Kirk of?

347 Hop Pole is a small Hamlet on the A16 road between Deeping St. James and?

348 What is the STD code for Little Ponton?

349 In the Civil War, the Battle of Winceby took place in which year?"

350 Rippingale railway station closed to passengers in?

351 What is the STD code for Holton cum Beckering?

352 Newark Golf course is at Beckingham. When was it founded?

353 Holton-le-Clay was a railway station on the East Lincolnshire Railway which served the villages of Holton-le-Clay and Tetney between 1848 and?

354 Bernie Taupin, the English lyricist famous for his collaboration with Elton John grew up in?

355 Huttoft is a small village, 4·5 miles east of the market town of?

356 Carlton-le-Moorland had a unique wooden post mill which blew down in?

357 Ingham is a village in the district of West Lindsey, located 14 km north of?

358 RAF Grimsby (Waltham) was initially opened as a satellite station for RAF Binbrook in November?

359 Mains sewerage provision finally arrived in Keal Cotes during?

360 Washingborough is a large village 3 miles east of?

361 The nearest town with schools and shops to East Stockwith is?

362 What is the post town for Helpringham?

363 Ludborough is a village in East Lindsey, notable for its railway station being the base for the heritage railway?

364 The Edward Richardson Primary School, Tetford, was founded via a bequest from Edward Richardson's will in?

365 What is the STD code for West Halton?

366 Lincoln Drill Hall was originally constructed as a military and police training hall in which year?

367 Uffington village lies 2 miles east of?

368 The nearest railway station for Brocklesby is?

369 Irby in the Marsh is a settlement on the B1195 East of Spilsby approximately 5 miles north of?

Fancy that!

Carlby: The churchyard is well kept with a variety of interesting tombstones including one finely carved and enriched with a cross and a memorial tablet that reminds us of the feeble grasp we all have on life because it announces that Oliver Smith "died suddenly in his chair" on May 21, 1872, aged 54 years: "In the midst of life we are in death".

370 Midville is a small village in the Lincolnshire Fens. The railway station closed in?

371 Which village has one of the oldest May poles in the kingdom?

372 Tallington is a small village situated 4 miles east of?

373 The former RAF Binbrook sergeants' mess is now?

374 It is rumoured that Thomas a Becket hid here during one of his arguments with King Henry II?

375 Where is the hamlet of Windsor in North Lincolnshire?

376 Where is the minor hamlet of Scotland?

377 Who commissioned the Dunston Pillar in 1751 as a navigational aid to assist those crossing the heathland around Dunston and Nocton?

378 Messingham is a small village outside?

379 Cranwell railway station, on a single track branch line from Sleaford, opened in?

380 Gedney Hill Golf Club is one of Lincolnshire's premier courses; it was designed in 1989 by?

381 What is the STD code for Lenton?

382 Tumby is a village located about 2 miles north of Coningsby and 6·5 miles south of?

383 RAF Wellingore opened in?

384 Bicker is a village on the A52, 9 miles west-south-west of?

385 Metheringham railway station closed to passengers on 11 September 1961 but it was later reopened on?

386 What was the World War II radar station situated near Donington on Bain?

387 Howell is a very small hamlet in North Kesteven near?

388 Marston is a village just north of the A1 near?

389 Keal Cotes windmill, built in the 18th century, fell into decay and disuse before being demolished in?

390 North Coates RAF airfield was built in?
391 Riseholme is the site of the rural science campus of the University of?
392 Tattershall Castle was built in 1434 by?
393 Walesby lies 3 miles north-east of Market Rasen and 7 miles south of?
394 Which town holds a regular Flower Parade?
395 Partney is a small village, around 3 miles north of?
396 Langworth's Boulters primary school closed in?
397 What is the STD code for Dyke?
398 Harrington is a small hamlet located 6 miles west of?
399 Burwell Priory was founded before 1110 by John de Hayes. Which religious order did it belong to?
400 Which long distance footpath passes through Grasby?
401 Rothwell church is dedicated to?
402 Swaby is situated about 8 miles north of Spilsby, and 6 miles north-west of?
403 Wainfleet All Saints is the birthplace of William of Wayneflete, Bishop of Winchester and founder of which college?
403 Magdalene College, Oxford.

404 Spalding Flower Bulb Museum was opened in 1995 at?
405 Marshchapel is a coastal village approximately 11 miles south-east of Grimsby and 13 miles north-east of?
406 A public elementary school was erected at Carlton-le-Moorland in?
407 RAF Elsham Wolds was re-opened with the arrival in July 1941 of?
408 Harmston is a small rural village 5 miles south of?
409 Little Steeping railway station closed in?
410 Ropsley was the birthplace of Richard Fox, the Tudor Bishop who funded which Oxford college?
411 Metheringham Delph drains into the River?
412 Rand is a small village approximately 9 miles north east of?
413 Torksey is a village on the eastern bank of the River?

Fancy that!

Stow Fair was a medieval fair inaugurated in 1233. Permission was granted in 1268 to the Prior of Sempringham for a fair here, confirming the earlier charter. This fair is known to have been held on the 23rd of June each year. But it seems likely that the earlier fairs were held on the same day, which is the feast day of St. Æthelreda, long associated with the site. The fair continued until living memory, being run as a Horse fair until 1954.

---

414 RAF Holbeach opened in?

415 Burton Pedwardine is a hamlet located 4·5 miles south-east of the market town of Sleaford and south-west of the village of?

416 Donington is located?

417 Owston Ferry lies on the west bank of the River?

418 Why is Minting is one of the Thankful Villages?

419 Rippingale station opened in 1871 for goods and closed in?

420 Bayons Manor at Tealby was demolished in?

421 Wragby is a small town approximately 10 miles north-west of Horncastle and about 11 miles from?

422 South Somercotes is a village 8 miles north-east of?

423 What is the STD code for Long Bennington?

424 The manor house, Burwell Park, was rebuilt in?

425 Novelist George Eliot used Gainsborough as her model for St. Ogg's in her book?

426 The quaint village of Hough-on-the-Hill lies approximately 7 miles due north of?

427 Fosse Way an important Roman route connects Lincoln with the city of?

428 Oasby is situated 6 miles from?

429 RAF Coleby Grange opened in?

430 Who founded Charterhouse School and Hospital in London?

431 Donington on Bain railway station served the village from 1875 to?

432 Why is Kirckstead's church named St Leonard's Without?

433 Great Hale church contains a hautbois, an early form of?

434 Burgh on Bain is a village about 7 miles west of?

435 Scopwick Tower Mill was built in 1827 and fell into disuse around?

436 The Victoria Hotel, Woodhall Spa, burned down on Easter Day?

437 Burton is a village in situated approximately 2 miles north of?

438 Firsby lies on the northern side of the waterway today known as the?

439 A former rector of Laceby church, John Whitgift, became Bishop of Worcester, was appointed as?

440 Glentworth is a village located 12 miles north of?

441 Which outdoor antiques fair has often featured on TVs *Bargain Hunt*?

442 When did Woodhall Spa railway station close?

443 Thornton Abbey railway station was built by the Great Grimsby and Sheffield Junction Railway in 1849, replacing one at?

444 Where is the tallest tower mill in the United Kingdom?

445 The LNER Class A4 4468 Mallard locomotive made its record-breaking run south through Little Bytham on?

446 The present Harlaxton Manor was built in?

447 RAF Digby was home to Hurricane and Spitfire squadrons and two famous pilots?

448 Haxey is a village situated 21·7 miles to the north-west of?

449 The Willoughby Memorial Library and Art Gallery at Corby Glen is housed in a 17th century building that was originally Reads Grammar School. The school was founded in?

450 Where is Knaith?

451 Toft Newton consists of the small villages of Toft next Newton, Newton by Toft and the hamlet of Newtoft. It is four miles west of?

452 RAF Scampton reopened in October?

453 The nearest town to Castle Bytham is?

454 Haconby is a small village 3 miles north of?

455 Where did the Lincolnshire Rising begin in 1536?

456 Fosdyke is a village 9 miles south of?

457 Blyton railway station opened in which year?

458 Bayons Manor at Tealby, was once owned by Charles Tennyson, later Tennyson d'Eyncourt, the uncle of?

459 Withcall is a small farming village 4 miles west of?

460 When did Skinnand become deserted?

461 What is the STD code for Moorby?

462 Humberston takes its name from a large boulder, the Humber Stone, which can still be seen at the entrance to?

Fancy that!

Northorpe. The village may also be famous for its wonderful shoe display competition which is held every July on the common green. Every year locals are given the chance to design a shoe. The village cobblers will produce shoes from the winning design. The fair has been under threat in recent years as the cobbler trade is struggling.

463 The pews inside Coleby church come from a former church at?

464 Great Ponton railway station was closed in?

465 Saxilby church is dedicated to?

466 Metheringham Methodist church was built in 1907 by the architect?

467 Following the fire at Stoke Rochford Hall, it was restored by English Heritage at a cost of?

468 Blyton Primitive Methodist chapel was built in?

469 Wrangle is a village 9 miles north-east of?

470 Which 15th century structure stands in Tattershall Market Place?

471 Martin is a small, ancient village just north of?

472 There was a telephone box at Coleby but it was removed in?

473 In which century was it decided that the steeple was unsafe and was taken down leaving Grasby church with just its square tower?

474 Which river passes through Easton?

475 Wragby is a small town approximately 10 miles north-west of Horncastle and about 11 miles from?

476 Where was Alfred, Lord Tennyson, the Poet Laureate, born and raised?

477 Maltby le Marsh is a between Alford and Mablethorpe. The village is at the junction of the A1104 and the?

478 Humberside International Airport was formerly?

479 Dunston is situated close to the B1188 road between Nocton to the north and?

480 Billy Butlin opened the UK's first holiday camp at Ingoldmells in?

481 Norton Disney is a small village situated between Lincoln and?

482 When did a light aircraft carrying 73 year old James Yates, of Martyr Worthy, crash in Ludford, killing the pilot.

483 What is the STD code for Irnham?

484 Burton-le-Coggles is a small village located south of?

485 RAF Station Fulbeck opened in?

486 Osgoodby is near to the A1103 and A46 two miles north-west of?

487 What speed did the Mallard locomotive make on its record-breaking run through Little Bytham?

488 What is the STD code for Kirkby on Bain?

489 Moulton Grammar School closed in?

490 Jubilee Park, Woodhall Spa, was opened in?

491 South Rauceby is a small village about 3 miles north-west of?

492 The Viking Way has passed through the south-east of Long Bennington since 1997 to avoid?

493 West Keal Primary School closed in which decade?

494 Lenton erected a splendid new lychgate to mark?

495 Irby upon Humber is a small village situated on the A46 road south-west of?

496 What is the post town for Langrick?

497 Fr. T. Pelham Dale SSC, vicar of Sausthorpe, was famous for having been prosecuted and imprisoned 1876 and 1880 for what crimes?

498 Owmby by Spital is a village 9 miles north of?

499 Where was the former RAF Binbrook station?

500 Next to the Church (in the grounds of Edlington Manor) archaeologists found evidence of?

501 Cranwell railway line was closed in?

502 Holton-le-Clay is twinned with?

503 In 1826 a fine, metre-long decorative shield was discovered in the River Witham. Now known as the Witham Shield it has been dated to 400-300 BC and is now in?

504 Great Hale is a small village, directly south of?

505 Thorpe Tilney Hall is to the south-west of Timberland. It was used as a setting for the BBC's 1980 *Pride and Prejudice* as?

506 Riseholme is a small village in the West Lindsey district about a mile north of?

Fancy that!

Woodhall Spa. The Kinema in the Woods situated in the centre of the Pinewoods is one of the treasures of Woodhall Spa and is completely unique. Housed in a converted cricket pavilion, when it opened in 1922 it was one of the first cinemas in Britain. It is one of the few cinemas in the country to still employ back projection and also offers regular entertainment on an original Compton Captain Organ. It is located next to the now derelict Spa Baths and opposite the site of the former Victoria Hotel.

507 617 Squadron was specifically established for the Dambusters mission and operated from?

508 Radio Lincolnshire briefly changed its name to BBC Radio Hemingby for one day on?

509 Elsham is the birthplace of the agricultural engineer?

510 Hemingby is a village in the East Lindsey district about 3 miles north of?

511 Saltfleetby has two old churches. What are they?

512 In 2002, West Farm on the Little Bytham road, Witham on the Hill, had trials for GM Rapeseed planted by?

513 When did a Canadian (RCAF) Avro Lancaster crash in the grounds of Stoke Rochford Hall?

514 Reads Grammar School in Corby Glen closed in?

515 Bracebridge Asylum (St John's Mental Hospital) closed down in?

516 The Heckington Show has been held annually in the village over the last weekend in July since?

517 Scotter is a large village situated between Scunthorpe and?

518 Scotter is a large village situated between Scunthorpe and?

519 The English Golf Union bought Woodhall Spa course in 1995 in order to set up?

520 Twenty is a small hamlet, 4 miles east of?

521 Moulton Grammar School was founded under the will of John Harrox (died 1561) who was steward to Sir John Harrington of Weston. The School opened in?

522 Where is the largest thatched manor house in England?

523 Easton Hall was pulled down in?

524 Harlaxton Manor is a popular location for filming. It was used in all the exterior shots and the Great hall for?

525 Edlington is a village located about 2 miles north-west of?

526 What day is the custom of Haxey Hood held?

527 What is the postal town for Lenton?

528 Mavis Enderby. Old Bolingbroke, it was the family seat of?

Fancy that!

Crowland is famous for its magnificent church, which forms part of the ruins of Croyland Abbey. Note the difference in spelling; the village is 'Crowland' and the abbey is 'Croyland'. This difference is probably down to as spelling mistake made by a medieval monk, but the mistake has stuck!

529 Whaplode Drove is approximately 10 miles south of?

530 The part of the Irish washerwoman Old Mother Riley was played by Arthur Lucan (born Arthur Towle). Where was he born?

531 What is the STD code for Owston Ferry?

532 Langrick is a small village in the Lincolnshire Fens, lying in?

533 Burton upon Stather is a village lying 5 miles north of the town of?

534 At 7 miles long, which is the longest village in the UK?

535 Keal Cotes is a small linear village on the A16 road one mile south of West Keal and one mile north of?

536 Where did Nancy Astor die in 1964?

537 What is the name of Irnham's Georgian inn?

538 On 27 February 2008 at 00·26 Ludford was at the epicentre of an earthquake measuring?

539 At Wilsthorpe, the old Peterborough Waterworks with its 52 ft deep artesian well drilled during the late 19th century provided how many gallons of water each day to supply the cathedral city 14 miles away?

540 Surfleet Railway Station closed to passengers in?

541 Where is the oak tree with the largest girth in the UK, with a circumference of forty feet?

542 Prominent in Greatford is Greatford Hall, a manor house built by Queen Elizabeth I in the 16th century. The Hall burned down in?

543 Colsterworth is a village and lies half a mile to the west of the A1 road, 7 miles south of Grantham and 13 miles north of?

544 Laceby church was restored in 1870 by?

545 Scawby church is dedicated to?

546 Welby is a village about 4·5 miles north-east of?

547 Thurlby Church is dedicated to?

548 What is the STD code for Reepham?

549 Blankney Cricket Club was originally formed in which year?

550 The "e" at the end of Humberstone was later dropped, to avoid confusion with another place of the same name?

551 Fulbeck is a small village in South Kesteven lying between Grantham and?

552 Scampton was the home of the Vulcan bomber during?

553 Ingoldsby is a small village in South Kesteven located 7 miles south-east of?

554 The first school was built at Ropsley in 1717. It was endowed by?

555 Gipsey Bridge School, Thornton Le Fen, was built in?

556 A mini-tornado swept through the Moulton, damaging the church roof and some other properties in the vicinity, depositing glass tens of metres away, on July 18 in which year?

557 What was the Lincolnshire Rising of 1536?

558 RAF Ludford Magna opened in?

559 In which year did Bardney railway station close?

560 In which year did Bardney railway station close?

561 Reepham is a small village north-east of?

562 Kyme Tower was a mediaeval castle which is believed to have been built between 1339 and 1381. Most of the building was demolished?

563 Threekingham Church is dedicated to?

564 In July 1977, more than fifty children from Branston junior school had to go to Lincoln County Hospital after?

565 Alford has a unique five sailed windmill, which dates from?

566 Carlton Scroop is a small village located 6 miles north-east of?

567 What is the STD code for Heckington?

568 Rippingale is a village on the A15 road about 5 miles north of?

569 Woodhall Spa is a village about 6 miles south-west of Horncastle and about 15 miles south-east-east of?

570 Long Bennington is twinned with the village of?

571 Silk Willoughby is a small village located 2 miles south of?

572 Moorby is a small village in East Lindsey with around fifty inhabitants. It is close to?

573 During World War II, RAF Ingoldmells was a?

574 Ludford primary school closed in?

575 Anton's Gowt is a hamlet approximately 2 miles north-west of the town of?

576 RAF Fiskerton opened in January 1943 as part of?

577 Saltfleetby is a village approximately 7 miles east of Louth, 10 miles north of?

578 Metheringham railway station was opened to passengers on 1 July of which year?

579 Stoke Rochford Golf Course was laid out in 1924 by the then owner?

580 Wilsford is a hamlet 5 miles west-south-west of Sleaford, and 9 miles north-east of?

581 Thurlby railway station was on the Bourne and Essendine railway, opened in 1860 and closed in?

582 Cranwell railway station building still stands and is in use as the current?

583 Scenes from the 1990 re-make of *Memphis Belle* were filmed at?

584 Which Deeping has an 18th century village lock-up?

585 What is the post town for Greatford?

586 Easton is a village just off the A1, north of?

587 Tathwell is a village around 3 miles south of?

588 Wellingore is a village 12 miles south of?

589 Tom Thumb, was just 47 cm tall and died in 1620, being buried in the parish church, aged 101. Tom Thumb's tiny house can be seen on the roof of another, larger house in the village. Where is it?

590 Little Humby is a small hamlet roughly 8 miles out of?

591 What is the post town for Haxey?

592 Kirkby on Bain lies on the River Bain between Horncastle and?

593 The King George V Swing Bridge near Althorpe connects the Isle of Axholme to?

594 RAF Coleby Grange closed just before the end of the war in May?

595 What is the postal town for Kirkby on Bain?

596 Four miles to the south of Mavis Enderby the Battle of Winceby occurred in?

Fancy that!

Cranwell: In 1682, Sir William and his wife Lady Anne Thorold are recorded as establishing a charity that gave about £8 and 2 shillings per year for the poor, to be distributed on Lady Day (25 March and then considered to be New Year's day). The parish also benefited from the will of Lady Margaret Thorold who granted £15 a year to apprentice four boys from the village. With the Poor Law Amendment Act reforms of 1834, the parish became part of the Sleaford Poor Law Union group of parishes.

Fancy that!

The most famous use of Greatford Hall was as the abode and private asylum for Dr. Francis Willis, an accomplished physician whose art was treatment of illustrious patients. It was he who cured King George III of his madness at Greatford Hall in 1788. It is not available for public viewing today.

597 Lenton is a small hamlet in the district of South Kesteven situated roughly 9·5 miles south east of?

598 Willoughton was a preceptory of the Knights Templar until their disbandment in?

599 Where was the birthplace of Herbert Ingram, founder of the *Illustrated London News*?

600 Salfleet Manor House was built in?

601 Moulton is situated between Spalding and?

602 Scawby Mill was opened about 1829 but the present tower was built as part of a house after the original tower collapsed during renovation work in?

603 The grass airfield at Dunholme was first used by the Royal Air Force during 1941 and 1942 for use by Handley Page Hampden aircraft from nearby?

604 Coleby is a hamlet in the civil parish of West Halton approximately 7 miles north of?

605 The RAF stayed at Elsham Wolds until?

606 Coleby Hall, a gabled house built for Sir William Lister (the father of Thomas Lister, the regicide) dates back to?

607 RAF East Kirkby opened on?

608 Ludford is a village and comprises the adjacent villages of Ludford Magna and?

609 Keadby is a small village lying just off the A18, west of?

610 Bloxholm church is dedicated to?

611 West Halton railway station was built by the North Lindsey Light Railway on 3 October?

612 Tetford is a village 6·5 miles north-east of Horncastle, 10 miles south of Louth and 8 miles north-west of?

613 Alfred Tennyson, 1st Baron Tennyson, FRS was born on 6 August 1809 and died?

614 Dame Sarah Ann Swift was born at Kirton Skeldyke on 22 November 1854. She died on 27 June 1937 and was a nurse and founder in 1916 of?

615 Tetford and its neighbour Salmonby hold an annual Scarecrow Festival in which month?

616 Kirton Brass Band was founded in?

617 Part of the Parris Island boot camp scenes for the 1987 film *Full Metal Jacket* were filmed at?

618 Willoughton is a village 13 miles north of?

619 Ashby de la Launde Hall was sold to Baron Garvagh. To keep his staff employed he built a large wooden indoor Badmington court which in later years became?

620 At what height above sea level does Great Gonerby stand?

621 RAF Scopwick was the first ever Royal Air Force airfield, being opened in?

622 The Manor Golf Club, situated 15 minutes from the centre of Grimsby on the A18 (Barton Street), was purchased by The Grimsby Institute in?

623 What is the STD code for South Ferriby?

624 The Three Kings Inn, Threekingham has been on the site since 871. Which ailing King stayed at the Inn during October 1216 when he was en route from Swineshead Abbey to Newark Castle where he died?

625 Welton is a village 7 miles north of?

626 Where did King John shelter after the infamous loss of his baggage train while crossing The Wash in 1216?

627 Morton and Hanthorpe is a civil parish formerly known as?

628 RAF East Kirkby is a former Royal Air Force base near the village of East Kirkby, south of Horncastle. What passes through the base?

629 What is unusual about Heckington Windmill?

630 Brocklesby is a village about four miles south-west of?

631 When did the GNR open Corby Glen railway station?

632 Which Roman road runs through West Deeping?

633 Kirton is on the A16 road, B1397 and B1192 south of Boston, near?

634 Willoughton Primitive Methodist church closed in?

635 When was RAF Swinderby put up for sale?

Fancy that!

617 Squadron was specifically established for the Dambusters mission codenamed 'Operation Chastise' in which Wing Commander Guy Gibson led the attack on the dams in the Ruhr Valley, for which he was awarded the Victoria Cross. The grave of his dog, Nigger, run over and killed the day before Operation Chastise, can still be seen at Scampton.

Fancy that!

Down Hall is a large red brick merchant's folly in Barrow upon Humber. Built in 1877 by JW Beeton, a willow merchant from Hull, the building originally served as both a grand house and Beeton's factory. Coal baskets, chairs, and prams were made. Beeton observed his workers from a glass tower on the roof of the building (removed some decades back), from which a panoramic view of the whole area could be seen.

Beeton was an eccentric character who paid his workers in distinctive octagonal tokens. It is alleged he lined the drive to Down Hall with skulls removed from a Saxon burial ground which was disturbed during building.

It was built by John Sleight of Barrow who said that the whole house was based on the calendar using the numbers seven, twenty-four, twelve, fifty-two and even three-hundred-and-sixty-five for numbers and measurements of doors, windows and other fittings. The builder claimed that the effort of building a house to such eccentric specifications almost killed him.

636 Rothwell is located approximately 10 miles to the south-west of Grimsby, and about 17 miles to the south-east of?

637 Salmonby village is 5·5 miles northeast of Horncastle, 10 miles south of Louth and 8 miles north-west of?

638 Spilsby is famous as the birthplace of the Arctic explorer Sir John Franklin, who was born here in?

639 Saxby All Saints parish church dates from 1849, and was designed by?

640 Who was the famous poet graduate of Louth Grammar School?

641 Fulbeck Hall has been the home of the Fane family since?

642 Deepings County Secondary Modern School was built in which year?

643 In which year did Oliver Cromwell win his first victory over the Royalists at Grantham?

644 British Railways closed Corby Glen station in?

645 Owston Ferry lies 9 miles north of?

646 The £2.5 million 2·8 mile-long Heckington village bypass, built by Reed & Mallik Ltd of Salisbury, was opened by Lynda Chalker, Baroness Chalker of Wallasey on?

647 Who did Margaret Hilda Roberts from Grantham become?

648 RAF Bardney, home to No.9 Squadron, opened on 13th April in which year?

649 Dowsby is a village in South Kesteven, lying on the western edge of the Fens. It is at the junction of the east-west B1397 and the north-south B1177. It is a mile north-east of Rippingale and just south of?

650 A brickworks north of Little Bytham, established in 1850 and active into the early 20th century, made small, high-fired paving bricks, called?

651 Silk Willoughby is a small village located 2 miles south of?

652 Scampton Church of England primary school dates from?

653 Timberland's village pub is called?

654 South Humber Bank Power Station at Stallingborough was built in?

655 Helen Fielding used the name "Mavis Enderby" in her 1996 novel?

656 Thornton Le Fen lies about 6 miles north of?

657 Who was the famous arctic explorer graduate of Louth Grammar School?

658 All Saints Church dominates Beckingham but is in a poor state of re pair. It was featured on the BBC TV programme *Restoration* in which year?

659 RAF Bracebridge Heath opened circa?

660 Dry Doddington is 6 miles from Newark and 9 miles from?

661 Somersby Manor was built by Sir John Vanbrugh, architect of Castle Howard, in?

662 What is the STD code for Sedgebrook?

663 Ropsley is a village about 5 miles east of?

664 RAF Metheringham was a bomber airfield during World War II. Opened in October 1943 and was decommissioned in the spring of?

665 Fantasy Island is a family Amusement Park in Ingoldmells. It opened in?

666 The first true school built in Cranwell opened in?

667 Harlaxton Manor was designed in 1837-1845 by?

668 East Halton is a small village close to the Humber Estuary. It is 10 miles from Barton-upon-Humber and 1 mile north of the neighbouring village?

669 When were three workers hurt after a toxic gas cloud escaped at the Cristal Global plant, North East Lincolnshire?

Fancy that!

Barholm church received a new tower during the English Civil War and the inscription records:

"Was ever such a thing
Since the Creation?
A new steeple built
In the time of vexation."

Fancy that!

A writer in *Notes and Queries* in 1932 noted that the place-name Busling-thorpe contains 13 different letters, exactly half the alphabet, none repeated and with no hyphenation, and wondered whether this was unique.

670 The station buildings in Surfleet stood until?

671 Waddington is a large village approximately 4 miles south of?

672 When did William Longespee and his wife Idonea apply for a Royal Charter to run a Friday market in Swaton?

673 The Grantham Canal passes 1·5 miles south-west of Sedgebrook. It opened in 1797 but closed in?

674 Oliver Cromwell is thought to have stayed at Saltfleet Manor House in 1643 before the battle of?

675 Kirmington is a village alongside the A18 road between Scunthorpe and?

676 Home Defence Flight Station Brattleby was renamed as Scampton in?

677 Castle Bytham and Little Bytham used to be called?

678 Who began the drainage of the marches around the Isle of Axholme in 1626?

679 Fiskerton is a small commuter village located approximately 6 miles east of?

680 Belton primary school that has been in existence since which year?

681 What is the STD code for Harlaxton?

682 Saxilby railway station, on the Doncaster to Lincoln Line was originally been built by?

683 Threekingham is a village on the A52 Grantham to Boston road, near?

684 Stoke Rochford Hall, designed by William Burn and built in 1845, was gutted by fire on 25 January?

685 Who was the poet, protestant martyr and the only woman on record to have been tortured in the Tower of London before being burnt at the stake born at Stallingborough?

686 Thornton Curtis is a village 5 miles south-east of?

687 A new secondary school opened in Corby Glen in?

688 The Foston Post Windmill was one of the oldest in Britain, dating back to 1624. It was demolished in?

689 The northern Cranwell airfield is the older, being used for light aircraft and airships from which year?

690 Sapperton is a hamlet located 1·5 miles from Ropsley. The nearest town is Grantham, which is 6 miles away. What is the post town?

691 In 1853 Irnham Hall was sold to Woodhouse and had several owners until bought by the present owners the Benton Jones family in?

692 Heckington railway station houses a railway museum. It was built in?

693 The first example of wallpaper was found in a bedroom at Saltfleet Manor House. A sample can be seen in?

694 RAF Swinderby was a Royal Air Force Bomber Command airfield opened in?

695 In 1643 Bolingbroke Castle was badly damaged in a siege during?

696 Great Gonerby is a large village less than 1 mile north of?

697 Which market place has a statue of the Arctic explorer Sir John Franklin?

698 Skinnand is a deserted medieval village situated 9 miles south of Lincoln and 11·5 miles north-west of?

Fancy that!

Byard's Leap is a small hamlet, west of Cranwell in Lincolnshire, associated with various legends, including the origin of the name.

The story goes that there was a witch called Old Meg, an evil crone who plagued the local villagers from her cave or hut in a spinney near the turning to Sleaford on Ermine Street, here called High Dike. She was a bane of the countryside and caused the crops to whither. A local champion, a retired soldier, came forward in response to the villagers' requests, and he asserted that he could kill her by driving a sword through her heart. To select a horse suitable for this task, he went to a pond where horses drank and dropped a stone in the pond, selecting the horse that reacted quickest, and this horse was known locally as 'Blind Byard', as he was blind.

The champion went to the witch's cave and called her out, but the witch refused, saying she was eating and he would have to wait. However, she crept up behind him and sank her long nails into the horse who ran, leaping over 60-foot. The champion regained control of the horse when they reached the pond, pursued by the witch, where he turned and thrust his sword into her heart, and she fell into the pond and drowned.

The spot where Blind Byard landed is marked by four posts in the ground with horseshoes on, and a commemorative stone. Byard's Leap is also associated with the activities of the Knights Templar, who allegedly held tournaments and jousts on the site. It lay at the southern end of their Temple Bruer military training ground.

699 Skellingthorpe and District Motorcycle Club was founded in?

700 Metheringham is a village 10 miles south of?

701 Sedgebrook had its own Primary School until?

702 Scopwick and Timberland railway station was on the line between Lincoln and Sleaford. It opened with the line in 1882 and closed in?

703 The Willoughby Arms, Little Bytham, is around 150 years old and was originally?

704 Kirkstead is a village on the River Witham and was amalgamated with the civil parish of Woodhall Spa in?

705 The medieval church of St Mary Magdalene at Gedney had 29 windows smashed in?

706 RAF Dunholme Lodge airfield was used by RAF Bomber Command during World War II and closed in?

707 Brant in Brant Broughton means?

708 Saltfleet is a coastal village approximately 8 miles north of Mablethorpe and 11 miles east of?

709 The Wesleyan Methodists built a small chapel at Humberston on Humberston Avenue in?

710 Donington On Bain Rovers Football Club was founded in?

711 In Spalding Market Place stands the White Hart Inn, which was built around 1377. Mary, Queen of Scots, stayed there in?

712 Where is the village of Bardney?

713 A National School was built in Foston next to the Church in?

714 Gunby Hall, near Spilsby, is a country house constructed in 1700. It is owned by?

715 South Kyme is a small village located 2·5 miles south-east of North Kyme which is itself 2·5 miles from?

716 The first commercial monorail in the UK opened at Ingoldmells Butlin's in?

717 In the early 17th Century, Sempringham was a centre of the Puritan movement in Lincolnshire. Samuel Skelton, vicar at the time, sailed to Massachusetts Bay in 1628 with the first group of Puritan settlers, who landed at?

718 Irnham is a village in South Kesteven about 10 miles south-east of?

719 What is the STD code for Burton upon Stather?

720 South Somercotes is a village 8 miles north-east of?

721 In 1959 the Dunholme Lodge airfield became a site for?

722 It is claimed that Lady Godiva was born here?

723 When did a RAF GR7 Harrier ZD430 of 3 Squadron travelling from RAF Leeming to Germany crash south-west of the village towards Burton Pedwardine?

724 Somersby is a village 6 miles north-west of Spilsby and 7 miles east-north-east of?

725 In which year did Bardney railway station open?

726 Humberston is home to a Tesco Extra store; which was expanded in 2006. A second floor was added in?

727 Where was Abigail Evelyn Titmuss, best known as Abi Titmuss, born 8 February 1976, a former glamour model, television personality and actress born?

728 Bucknall is a village about 7 miles west of?

729 Sedgebrook Grammar School was erected in 1882 and by 1913 it was a Secondary School. It was absorbed into The King's School, Grantham, in?

730 Tetney is on the A1031 road, the Cleethorpes-Mablethorpe road, just south of Cleethorpes and Humberston. A mile to the west is?

731 If you look carefully on the northern side of St Mary's Church, Barnetby, a crude carving of which animal can be seen?

732 RAF Harlaxton closed in?

733 Boston. The settlers who founded Boston, Massachusetts sailed from here in?

Fancy that!

Laceby's only pub is the Laceby Arms, originally two separate establishments known as the Waterloo Inn and the Nags Head Inn which were noted in the *Guinness Book of Records* at one time as the two closest pubs in England. They were joined into one establishment in 1990. After a period of closure the Laceby Arms re-opened on 22 March 2009 after a new landlord bought the premises.

Fancy that!

Several media stunts have associated themselves with the name of Twenty, in the past few decades; most notably by *The Sun* newspaper around its 20p price. Its inhabitants too, have a sense of humour. For example, its horizon is as wide as the sea's – so a regulation pattern road sign appeared, declaring that Twenty had been twinned with the Moon. Across this had been spray-painted the legend – "no atmosphere".

734 Where are the RAF's Red Arrows based?

735 Dyke is a hamlet in the civil parish of?

736 Surfleet primary school was built in?

737 In 1715, Robert Bertie, the 16th Baron Willoughby de Eresby, employed who to design a baroque front to the house to celebrate his ennoblement as the first Duke of Ancaster and Kesteven?

738 Brookenby is a village situated 9 miles north-east of?

739 What is the STD code for Barnetby?

740 Scothern is a small village situated 6 miles north-east of?

741 Foston School was closed in?

742 The Viking Way passes through Barnetby as it makes its way from the River Humber to?

743 Barkston is a small village lying on the A607 three miles north of?

744 Firsby railway station opened in?

745 Where was the birthplace of Henry IV?

746 Donington on Bain lies about six miles south-west of?

747 During World War II the Butlin's Ingoldmells camp was used as the site of?

748 Saxilby is a large village about 6 miles north-west of?

749 Barnetby lies between Scunthorpe and?

750 In 2002, scenes from *Dolly's Brood* were filmed at?

751 Heckington is located about midway between Sleaford and?

752 RAF Sandtoft, near Belton, a former RAF Bomber Command base closed in which year?

753 Althorpe is twinned with which other parish?

754 In which year were medieval wall paintings found in Corby Glen parish church?

756 Skellingthorpe is a large village located 4 miles south-west of?

757 Donington on Bain sits on the east bank of the?

758 Where did Oliver Cromwell fight his first battle?

759 Scawby is located 3 miles SW of?

760 St Mary's Church, Barnetby, had the only lead font in the county. Where is it now?

761 Bulby is a hamlet located north of the town of?

762 St Andrew's parish church, Firsby, was rebuilt in 1856 by architect?

763 Bothertoft Parish Church is dedicated to . Gilbert of Sempringham. When was it built?

764 Scampton is 4 miles north of?

765 Bratoft is a small hamlet lying west of?

766 Where is the largest trolleybus museum in Europe?

767 Billingborough is a village about 10 miles north of Bourne and 10 miles south of?

768 After the end of the Second World War in Blankey Cricket Club went into decline and closed a few years later. When was it re-formed?

769 Grimsthorpe is a village about four miles north-west of?

770 At the start of the Second World War Blankey Hall was requisitioned for use as billets for servicemen from nearby RAF stations. During 1945 it was badly damaged by fire and was then left as an empty shell before being demolished in which decade?

771 Surfleet is a small village situated on the River Glen about 5 miles north of?

772 When were the council houses built on land at Brothertoft?

773 South Ferriby is a village situated on the south bank of the Humber Estuary 3 miles west of?

774 Dr. Thomas Hurst was born in Barrowby in 1598 and became rector of the village in 1629. He was chaplain to?

Fancy that!

Woodhall Spa came about by accident in 1811 after John Parkinson, of Old Bolingbroke made several attempts to find coal. After spending several thousand pounds, and sinking a shaft over 1,000 feet deep, the enterprise was abandoned on account of the now rising spring. The spring flows daily through soft spongy rock, at a depth of 520 feet.

About 1834, the then Lord of the Manor, Thomas Hotchkin Esquire, ascertained by analysis that the water was in fact valuable, being an iodine containing mineral spring. He spent nearly £30,000 sinking the well and erecting the Spa baths, and the Victoria Hotel.

In 1886 the estate was purchased by a syndicate and extensive alterations and improvements were made. The entry for the Spa in *Kellys Directory of Lincolnshire*, dated 1919, claims there were 56 different types of treatment at the Spa.

Fancy that!

Back in 1751 the eccentric nobleman Sir Francis Dashwood had a 92 foot high column erected at Dunston to act as a lighthouse on land for travelers. The lantern, popularly called the Dunston Pillar, was replaced by a statue of George III to mark that monarch's Jubilee, but the statue was later taken down after it proved to be a danger to low flying aircraft.

775 Firsby is a small village south-east of the nearest market town of Spilsby and 8 miles inland from the popular holiday resort town of?

776 Belton is noteworthy for the Grade 1 listed Belton House completed in which year?

777 For many years Barrow on Humber supported a mummers troupe known as the Plough-Jags. Such troupes were associated with the festivities of?

778 Described as the most complete example of a typical English country house – where is it?

779 Braceborough Spa had a bath house was built in 1841. Which king did Doctor Willis treat here for his madness?

780 Sedgebrook is a village 4 miles west of?

781 Braceborough Spa finally closed in?

782 Where was the founder of The Samaritans, Reverend Prebendary Edward Chad Varah's father born?

783 Althorpe is a small village lying on the A18 four miles west of?

784 First built in 1640, Hickson's Almshouses at Barkston were rebuilt in which year?

785 A local government reform in 1996 abolished?

786 The United Lincolnshire Hospitals NHS Trust is one of the largest trusts in the country, employing 4,000 staff and with an annual budget of over?

787 The 'Skegness is so Bracing' poster featuring The Jolly Fisherman helped to put Skegness on the map and is now world famous. The poster was derived from an oil painting by?

788 Market days in Market Rasen are Tuesdays, Fridays and?

789 Grantham is also notable for having the first female police officers in the United Kingdom, in which year?

790 A weekly market is held in Alford Corn Exchange every?

791 A great annual horse fair was held at Horncatle from the 13th century. In the 19th century was probably the largest event of its kind in the United Kingdom. But the last fair was held in?

792 What is the STD code for Chapel St Leonards?

793 A Time Team excavation in 2002 revealed a cist bearing an inscription to the God?

794 The Grimmsby Dock Tower was completed in?

795 Between the years 1307 and 1311 the central tower of Lincon Cathedral was raised to its present height of ?

796 Lincolnshire was historically associated with the Lincolnshire bag pipe, noted as very popular in the county. The last player, John Hunsley of Middle Manton died in?

797 The Newby Wyke Brewery is based in?

798 The Lincolnshire Agricultural Society was formed in?

799 During the filming of *The Da Vinci Code* in Lincoln Cathedral, Tom Hanks and many of the leading cast stayed at the nearby

800 BBC Radio Lincolnshire broadcasts on?

Fancy that!

Horncastle. The Romans had a fort here which they called Banovallum. The parish church contains a brass memorial to the King's Champion of 1519. This was a hereditary post held by the Dymoke family, who had the right to ride fully armed to the coronation of a monarch and challenge anyone to contest the new monarch's right to the throne. Also in the church are a collection of scythes used as weapons at the battle of Winceby in 1643.

Answers

1 Quarrying and masonry.
2 Stamford on the B1176.
3 South Kesteven.
4 Grantham.
5 1959.
6 1877. It is still in operation.
7 1645.
8 Lindum Colonia, or more fully, Colonia Domitiana Lindensium, after its founder Domitian.
9 1660.
10 Bourne.
11 Thursdays.
12 Oliver Cromwell.
13 01522.
14 Spalding.
15 It is a village in North Kesteven. One of the earliest references to Jerusalem was found in documents dating back to 1436.
16 Stephen.
17 North west of Alford.
18 1946.
19 Sir Isaac Newton.
20 Market Rasen.
21 Mondays.
22 1290.
23 2005.
24 Bourne.
25 1856.
26 Spalding.
27 868.
28 01400.
29 Tongue End between Baston, Bourne, and Pode Hole.
30 Louth.
31 2006.
32 Witham to the west and south.
33 Grimsby and 2 miles west of the A18 road. It neighbours the small village of Beelsby.
34 1964.
35 1884.
36 The 1951 Festival of Britain.
37 1947.
38 Lincoln, just off the A15 and near Caenby Corner.
39 William le Gros, the Earl of Yorkshire.
40 Cleethorpes.
41 1965.
42 Scunthorpe, on the B1207 road.
43 1238.
44 Sir Cecil Wray.
45 01775.
46 Scunthorpe.
47 John Ruskin (8 February 1819 – 20 January 1900).
48 1538.
49 A group of round barrows dating back to the Bronze Age.
50 1995.
51 1986.
52 The club play at the 10,120-capacity Sincil Bank.
53 An earthquake.
54 Skegness.
55 North Somercotes.
56 The city of Lincoln, reputedly the oldest arch in the United Kingdom still used by traffic.
57 It hardened immediately after quarrying, making it suitable for both building and artistic carving.
58 Cleethorpes.
59 1810.
60 Melton High Wood next to the A180 main road.
61 1872.
62 RAF Cranwell.
63 01476.
64 Landing lights for the nearby RAF Waddington airbase.
65 Lincoln.
66 1894.
67 King George V Swing Bridge.
68 Boston.

69 Dorchester.

70 Conningsby.

71 Lincoln just east of the A15.

72 Cadwell Park.

73 Great Coates.

74 01724.

75 1852.

76 Sleaford.

77 Lincoln Castle.

78 Hull.

79 4 miles north of Bourne in the District of South Kesteven.

80 They were killed by lightning in 1830.

81 RAF Cammeringham.

82 On Saturday 1 June 1974 at 16:53.

83 Grantham.

84 Empress Matilda, led by her illegitimate half brother Robert, 1st Earl of Gloucester.

85 1216.

86 1916.

87 Till, a small river whose lower reaches form the Fossdyke Navigation.

88 In the redundant church at Kingerby, a small hamlet near Market Rasen.

89 Heckington.

90 River Bain.

91 Sleaford.

92 1014.

93 Matthew Flinders.

94 1185.

95 2006.

96 Skegness.

97 1816 and the Hall Farm's farmhouse was erected on the site.

98 01406.

99 1996.

100 Thurlby.

101 1984.

102 1916.

103 St. Mary's, Marshchapel.

104 1980.

105 North of Stamford on the B1176.

106 1967.

107 William Byrd (1540 or late 1539 – 4 July 1623).

108 The River Witham.

109 South Thoresby.

110 Crowle on the A161, near the junction with the A18.

111 1951, and goods traffic on 17 December 1956.

112 Holbeach.

113 Skegness.

114 The Everett family.

115 1981.

116 Hibaldstow.

117 Boston, on the A52 road.

118 Spalding.

119 Market Rasen.

120 Fr. T. Pelham Dale SSC.

121 1848 for the Great Northern Railway by J H Taylor.

122 Lincoln, just off the A15.

123 Cherry Willingham.

124 John Harrison whose expertise at designing marine chronometers allowed navigators to successfully calculate longitude at sea.

125 The "long drop" system of execution.

126 Two 6th century French saints.

127 Bateman's Brewery.

128 Lincoln.

129 Ermine Street.

130 01526.

131 Colsterworth.

132 Market Rasen.

133 Just outside Stamford.

134 Owston Ferry.

135 1961.

136 The National Trust.

137 1953.

138 Lincoln.

139 Radegund (c. 520–586) was a 6th century Frankish princess, who founded the monastery of the Holy

Cross at Poitiers. Canonized in the 9th century, she is the patron saint of several English churches and of Jesus College, Cambridge.

140 01754.

141 Seven monasteries.

142 1848.

143 Sleaford.

144 Anwick.

145 Australia.

146 Boston.

147 1549.

148 "The Little Boys' Ashby". This came about after the bishop assigned the revenues of the vicarage of Ashby to the upkeep of the boys in the cathedral choir.

149 Benedictine.

150 Boston.

151 01476.

152 HMP Morton Hall, a women's semi-open prison holding a high percentage of foreign nationals.

153 Mansfield Wilkinson of Louth.

154 Sir John Houblon who was the first governor of the Bank of England.

155 Sleaford, just off the A15.

156 Mark Faviell.

157 A stone tower and a former 'land lighthouse'. It stands beside the A15 road approximately 6 miles south of Lincoln near the junction of the B1178.

158 Lincoln.

159 01724.

160 RAF Conningsby.

161 St. Vedast, Bishop of the Frankish Church died c540.

162 Fulbeck.

163 1944.

164 Barton-upon-Humber.

165 Graham Taylor, who managed the English national football team from 1990 to 1993.

166 The superb 15th century church of St James, Louth.

167 1 July 1882 named Blankney & Metheringham.

168 The city of Lincoln.

169 St Germain.

170 Barton-upon-Humber.

171 1955.

172 Bag Enderby.

173 1863.

174 Ancaster.

175 Louth.

176 c870.

177 Lincoln.

178 74.

179 A new fountain.

180 Keal Cotes.

181 Horncastle.

182 South Kesteven.

183 1970.

184 Lincoln.

185 2008.

186 1952 and to goods in 1964.

187 Wrawby.

188 01529.

189 1891. Closed in the 1950s the building still stands and is now used as general storage facility by a local farmer.

190 February 1221.

191 Lincoln.

192 Lincoln. A Norman building on Steep Hill immediately above Jew's House, it is dated to between 1150 and 1180 and is a Grade I listed building.

193 Because it lost no men in World War I.

194 Spalding.

195 A Kingfisher.

196 Woolsthorpe-by-Colsterworth.

197 An earthquake.

198 Horncastle some eight miles to the north.

199 Tetford.

200 A water-pipe under the ground. A

sewer. A flood-gate, through which the marsh-water runs from the reens into the sea.

201 The former steeple collapsed.

202 1857 for the Royal North Lincoln Militia.

203 Bourne on the A151.

204 The millennium.

205 Trent.

206 Kesteven and West Lindsey.

207 01427.

208 1998.

209 Horncastle.

210 Mablethorpe.

211 1697.

212 December 1916.

213 01526.

214 St George's Academy.

215 1976.

216 It was opened in September 2006.

217 Saint Hybald, a 7th century Saxon saint, who died circa 690.

218 Lincoln.

219 Boston.

220 The Lincolnshire Wildlife Trust.

221 Market Rasen.

222 1972.

223 1964.

224 1867.

225 1979.

226 1539.

227 Newark-on-Trent.

228 Anwick.

229 01754.

230 Billingborough.

231 Witham, about three miles to the east of its source.

232 30.

233 Spilsby.

234 The Battle on Gonerby Moor.

235 1828.

236 Lincoln.

237 1726.

238 1975.

239 Waring.

240 Sir Christopher Wray (1524 – 7 May 1592).

241 1924.

242 Winteringham.

243 01205.

244 Deeping St James.

245 The Everett family.

246 Its dramatic leaning spire.

247 Saint-Rémy-de-Sillé in Sarthe, whose main road has been renamed Rue de Grasby.

248 1890.

249 4 houses and a church.

250 Eagle, near Swinderby.

251 1970.

252 1954.

253 Horncastle.

254 01400.

255 Lincoln, just north of the A46.

256 1959.

257 Welton le Marsh.

258 Spilsby.

259 1723.

260 Lincoln.

261 The National Trust.

262 Anwick.

263 Bourne. It is sandwiched between Little Bytham and Swinstead.

264 01775.

265 Lincoln.

266 1951.

267 Spilsby, some six miles to the north.

268 Causennae.

269 King Henry IV on 3 April 1367.

270 Grantham.

271 Barton-upon-Humber.

272 1918.

273 Huttoft.

274 Grantham.

275 Grimsby.

276 Skirbeck, the mill only ceased working in 1932.

277 01522.

278 Grimsby.

279 Edward King.

280 1970.

281 English Heritage.

282 Digby.

283 The Bishop of Grimsby.

284 Aswarby Hall.

285 Grantham.

286 01790.

287 1940.

288 Grantham.

289 A few metres south of Julian's Bower, Alkborough.

290 Scunthorpe.

291 1802.

292 Lady Godiva.

293 The First World War.

294 Ballon, in the Sarthe department of France.

295 Gunby St. Nicholas.

296 1536.

297 Market Deeping.

298 It is pronounced hee not hay.

299 The Auld South Yorkshire.

300 The Trolleybus Museum at Sandtoft. It is located on the site of the former RAF Sandtoft, which also includes Sandtoft Airfield.

301 Humberside Airport.

302 1972.

303 1848.

304 The British Library.

305 56.

306 1903. He returned there after the trauma of the Great War and began writing *The Middle Parts of Fortune*.

307 1848.

308 Knaith.

309 Bourne.

310 1139 by Hugh Brito, lord of Tattershall.

311 Lincoln.

312 Spilsby and 137 miles from London.

313 1904.

314 Louth.

315 1968.

316 Bourne.

317 St. Peter's, Markby.

318 The 1970s.

319 Sleaford. It became part of the parish of Scopwick in 1931.

320 Near Bardney Abbey.

321 Lincolnshire County Council.

322 St. Martin.

323 Louth.

324 Barkston.

325 Sir Charles Thorold.

326 South Killingholme.

327 The Frances Olive Anderson School.

328 The sewage works at Marston.

329 Grimsby.

330 1989.

331 01205.

332 The Gunpowder Plot.

333 1530.

334 Lincoln. He died 22 June 2009.

335 Bradley, near Grimsby.

336 Capability Brown.

337 Lincoln.

338 Sandilands, Sutton on Sea. The tournament takes place at the Grange and Links hotel and on a number of private courts in the village.

339 The Burghley Arms on the Market Square.

340 1959.

341 1874 and 1876.

342 1990.

343 B1241, approximately 2 miles south of Gainsborough and 14 miles north-west of Lincoln.

344 Sir John Nelthorpe.

345 The University of Evansville's British campus. Students from universities throughout the United States stay at Harlaxton while spending a semester studying abroad.

346 1945.

347 Sleaford.

348 1916.

349 Lavington.

350 Alford.

351 The Queen of the Fens.

352 2001.

353 Ruskington.

354 Grantham.

355 01778.

356 The Curry Inn.

357 Stamford.

358 1841.

359 1956.

360 The National Trust.

361 Edward Milner.

362 John Harrison who won £20,000 for inventing the marine chronometer.

363 RAF Scampton.

364 Grantham, just off the A1.

365 01775.

366 1873.

367 Alford.

368 1884 and 1886.

369 Albert Edward Lambert.

370 Robinson Crusoe.

371 Polycarp (A.D. 69 – A.D. 155) was a second century Christian bishop of Smyrna.He died a martyr, bound and burned at the stake then stabbed when the fire failed to touch him. He is regarded as a saint in the Roman Catholic, Eastern Orthodox, Oriental Orthodox, Anglican, and Lutheran Churches.

372 1945.

373 1916.

374 1970.

375 "Muddy dump". It is also known as "death's fen".

376 Brigsley.

377 20 January 2008.

378 Alkborough.

379 Spilsby.

380 Lincoln line.

381 A Hurricane.

382 1941.

383 2009.

384 The Limelight Theatre.

385 Scunthorpe,

386 John Harrington, the eldest son of Sir Sapcote(s) Harrington of Rand.

387 North Kelsey Beck.

388 Horncastle. It is a corruption of Malbis Enderby, taken from the name of 14th century French land-holders.

389 1951.

390 Gainsborough.

391 Grantham.

392 Raithby by Spilsby.

393 Newport Arch in Lincoln.

394 Brigg.

395 01724.

396 RAF Scopwick.

397 The RAF in 1946.

398 1,000 acres.

399 Bourne.

340 Robert (Mouseman) Thompson (also known as Mousey Thompson) of Kilburn.

341 Scunthorpe.

342 The imposing tower of Boston's parish church, dedicated to St Botolph.

343 St. Margaret of Antioch.

344 Immingham.

345 Oakham and Uppingham in Rutland.

346 Sleaford.

347 Deeping St. Nicholas.

348 01476.

349 1643, when the Royalist army was defeated by the Roundheads at "Slash Hill".

350 1930.

351 01673.

352 1901.

353 1964.

354 Owmby by Spital.

355 Alford.

356 The 1930s.

357 Lincoln on the B1398.

358 1941.

359 1994 although a mains gas supply has never been available,

360 Lincoln.

361 Gainsborough, three miles away.

362 Sleaford.

363 Lincolnshire Wolds Railway.

364 1714.

365 01724.

366 1890.

367 Stamford.

368 Habrough.

369 Wainfleet.

370 1970.

371 Hemswell.

372 Stamford.

373 Brookenby Church.

374 Haverholme Priory.

375 It is attached to the town of Crowle.

376 Near Ingoldsby.

377 Sir Francis Dashwood (better known as the founder of the Hellfire Club).

378 Scunthorpe.

379 1917 and served the naval aviation training facility then known as RNAS Daedalus, later to become RAF Cranwell.

380 Charles Britton.

381 01476.

382 Horncastle.

383 1935.

384 Boston.

385 6 October 1975.

386 RAF Stenigot.

387 Ewerby.

388 Long Bennington.

389 1949.

390 1916.

391 Lincoln.

392 Ralph de Cromwell, 3rd Baron Cromwell – Henry VI's Lord High Treasurer.

393 Caistor.

394 Spalding.

395 Spilsby.

396 1989, when its pupils transferred to the newly-built Ellison Boulters School in neighbouring Scothern.

397 01778.

398 Alford, covering just over 1000 acres.

399 Benedictine.

400 The Viking Way.

401 St Mary Magdelene.

402 Alford.

403 Magdalene College, Oxford.

404 Pinchbeck.

405 Louth.

406 1854.

407 103 Squadron.

408 Lincoln.

409 1970.

410 Corpus Christi College.

411 Witham.

412 Lincoln.

413 Trent.

414 1926.

415 Heckington.

416 8 miles from Spalding, on the A152.

417 Trent.

418 They suffered no fatalities during the Great War of 1914 to 1918.

419 1964.

420 1964.

421 Lincoln.

422 Louth and around 2 miles south of North Somercotes.

423 01400.

424 1760.

425 *The Mill on the Floss.*

426 Grantham.

427 Leicester and the south-west of England.

428 Grantham.

429 1939.

430 Thomas Sutton b.1532 in Knaith.

431 1951.

432 It was outside the gates of the abbey.

433 The oboe.

434 Louth.

435 1912, It remains standing.

436 1920.

437 Lincoln.

438 Steeping River.

439 Archbishop of Canterbury by Queen Elizabeth I. He had been born near Grimsby in 1530.

440 Lincoln.

441 Swinderby.

442 1971.

443 Thornton Curtis.

444 Moulton.

445 3 June 1938.

446 1837.

447 Douglas Bader and Guy Gibson.

448 Lincoln.

449 1669.

450 2 miles from Gainsborough.

451 Market Rasen.

452 1936.

453 Stamford.

454 Bourne.

455 The church of St James, Louth.

456 Boston on the A16 and A17.

457 1848.

458 Alfred, Lord Tennyson.

459 Louth.

460 During the English Civil War of 1642-1646, when the church fell into ruins.

461 01507.

462 The village library.

463 Hackthorn.

464 1959.

465 St Botolph.

466 Albert Edward Lambert.

467 £12m over three years.

468 1851.

469 Boston.

470 The buttercross.

471 Timberland.

472 2008.

473 The 19th century.

474 The River Witham.

475 Lincoln.

476 Somersby.

477 A157.

478 RAF Kirmington.

479 Metheringham to the south.

480 1936.

481 Newark.

482 On 9 October 1994.

483 01476 55.

484 Grantham.

485 1940.

486 Market Rasen.

487 126 mph.

488 01526.

489 1939.

490 1937.

491 Sleaford.

492 A direct crossing of the A1.

493 1960s.

494 The Millennium.

495 Laceby.

496 Boston.

497 Ritualist practices and regarded as a martyr by Anglo-Catholics. He was the parish priest from 1881-1892 and is buried in the churchyard.

498 Lincoln just off the A15.

499 Brookenby.

500 A small Roman camp where they found pots of oxen bones, most likely used for ceremonial purposes.

501 1956.

502 Sargé-lès-le-Mans, Sarthe, France.

503 The British Museum.

504 Heckington.

505 Longbourn Hall.

506 Lincoln.

507 RAF Scampton.

508 April 18 2007.

509 Richard Hornsby born 1790. By 1840, his company made steam engines, which were used for traction engines.

510 Horncastle.

511 All Saints (redundant) and St Peter's of which only the tower remains.
512 Aventis.
513 28 April 1945.
514 1909.
515 1990.
516 1864.
517 Gainsborough.
518 Gainsborough.
519 A National Golf Centre.
520 Bourne.
521 1562.
522 Alford. It is dated 1611.
523 1951.
524 *The Haunting,* as well as interior and exterior shots in the films *The Ruling Class, The Lady and the Highwayman,* and *The Last Days of Patton.* It was also used to film the BBC drama *The Young Visitors.* Most recently it was used as the setting for *Australian Princess.*
525 Horncastle.
526 6th January.
527 Grantham.
528 John of Gaunt.
529 Spalding.
530 Sibsey.
531 01427.
532 Langriville parish.
533 Scunthorpe,
534 Deeping St. Nicholas.
535 Stickford.
536 Grimsthorpe Castle.
537 The Griffin.
538 5·2 on the Richter scale.
539 One million!
540 1961 and to goods in 1963.
541 The Bowthorpe Oak, Bowthorpe Park Farm, Manthorpe.
542 1930 and was subsequently rebuilt in a similar style to the original.
543 Stamford.
544 James Fowler, architect of Louth.
545 St. Hybald, a 7th century Saxon.
546 Grantham.
547 St Firman.
548 01522.
549 1873.
550 Humberstone in Leicestershire.
551 Lincoln.
552 The Cold War.
553 Grantham.
554 James Thompson.
555 1859.
556 2005.
557 A short revolt against Henry VIII's establishment of the Church of England and his Dissolution of the Monasteries.
558 June 1943.
559 1970.
560 1970.
561 Lincoln.
562 1720 – 1725 leaving only the single ashlar (stone block) tower.
563 St. Peter ad Vincula (St. Peter in chains).
564 A crop spraying aircraft inadvertently sprayed their play-ground.
565 1839.
566 Grantham.
567 01529.
568 Bourne.
569 Lincoln.
570 Bretteville l'Orgueilleuse in Normandy, France.
571 Sleaford.
572 Wood Enderby.
573 Chain Home Low radar station, providing low-altitude short-range warning.
574 2009.
575 Boston.
576 5 Group, RAF Bomber Command.
577 Mablethorpe.
578 1882.
579 Christopher Turnor.

580 Grantham.
581 1951.
582 RAF main guardroom.
583 RAF Binbrook.
584 Deeping St. James.
585 Stamford.
586 Woolsthorpe-by-Colsterworth and Colsterworth in South Kesteven.
587 Louth.
588 Lincoln.
589 Tattershall.
590 Grantham. There is also Great Humby about ½ a mile down the road, which is actually smaller.
591 Doncaster.
592 Coningsby just west of the A153.
593 Scunthorpe.
594 1945.
595 Woodhall Spa.
596 1643.
597 Grantham.
598 1312.
599 Swineshead.
600 1511 although some parts are believed to date back to 1347.
601 Holbeach.
602 1994.
603 RAF Scampton.
604 Scunthorpe.
605 June 1918, the wooden huts and a small aircraft shed were demolished by 1919.
606 1628.
607 20 August 1943.
608 Ludford Parva.
609 Scunthorpe.
610 St Mary.
611 1906.
612 Spilsby.
613 6 October 1892.
614 The Royal College of Nursing, and introduced nurse registration.
615 May.
616 1870.
617 Swinderby.

618 Lincoln.
619 The present Village Hall, relocated today in the centre of the village.
620 360ft.
621 March 1918.
622 2007.
623 01652.
624 King John.
625 Lincoln.
626 The Cistercian abbey in Swineshead.
627 Morton by Bourne.
628 The Greenwich meridian.
629 It is the only 8-sailed example of its type still standing in Europe. The tower windmill built as a five-sailed mill in 1830 and turned into an eight-sailed mill after serious storm damage in 1890/2.
630 Immingham.
631 1853.
632 King Street.
633 Frampton and Sutterton.
634 1979.
635 1995.
636 Scunthorpe.
637 Spilsby.
638 1786.
639 George Gilbert Scott.
640 Alfred, Lord Tennyson.
641 1632.
642 1958.
643 1643.
644 1959.
645 Gainsborough.
646 14 December 1982.
647 Margaret Thatcher.
648 1943.
649 Pointon.
650 Adamantine Clinkers (because of their hardness).
651 Sleaford.
652 1870.
653 The Pennyfarthing.
654 1997.

655 *Bridget Jones's Diary.*
656 Boston.
657 Sir John Franklin.
658 2006.
659 1919-1920.
660 Grantham.
661 1722.
662 01949.
663 Grantham.
664 1946.
665 1995.
666 1850.
667 Anthony Salvin, but was replaced by William Burn, who is responsible for its interior detailing.
668 North Killingholme.
669 5 March 2010.
670 1994 when they were bulldozed to make way for the building of the A16 Spalding Bypass.
671 Lincoln.
672 1240.
673 1936.
674 Winceby.
675 Grimsby.
676 1917.
677 West and East Bytham.
678 Vermuyden.
679 Lincoln.
680 1869.
681 01476.
682 The Great Northern and Great Eastern Joint Railway.
683 Sleaford.
684 2005.
685 Anne Askew (1520/1521 - 1546).
686 Barton-upon-Humber.
687 1963.
688 1966.
689 1916.
690 Sleaford.
691 1901.
692 1859.
693 The V & A museum in London.
694 1940.

695 The Battle of Winceby.
696 Grantham.
697 Spilsby.
698 Sleaford.
699 Spring 2001.
700 Lincoln.
701 1981.
702 1955.
703 The booking office and waiting room for a private railway.
704 1987.
705 2006, including a 14th century Jesse window, vestments and an altar cloth were set alight but luckily the fire did not take hold. A 15-year-old and a 16-year-old were interviewed by police and admitted causing the damage.
706 1964.
707 Burnt.
708 Louth.
709 1835. A larger, replacement chapel was built in 1907.
710 1948.
711 1566.
712 10 miles east of Lincoln.
713 1847.
714 The National Trust.
715 Billinghay.
716 1965.
717 Salem.
718 Grantham.
719 01724.
720 Louth and around 2 miles south of North Somercotes.
721 Bloodhound surface-to-air missiles with 141 Squadron until it was disbanded and the station finally closed in 1964.
722 Bucknall.
723 On 28 June 1993. The pilot ejected safely, having ejected at 3,000 ft.
724 Horncastle.
725 1848.
726 2007.

727 Ruskington.
728 Horncastle.
729 1919.
730 Holton-le-Clay.
731 A cat.
732 1957.
733 1630.
734 RAF Scampton.
735 Bourne.
736 1878.
737 Sir John Vanbrugh. It is his last masterpiece.
738 Market Rasen.
739 01652.
740 Lincoln.
741 1987.
742 Oakham, in Rutland.
743 Grantham.
744 1850.
745 Bolingbroke Castle.
746 Louth.
747 HMS Royal Arthur, a Royal Navy shore establishment.
748 Lincoln.
749 Grimsby.
750 RAF Binbrook.
751 Swineshead Bridge south of the A17 road.
752 1955.
753 Keadby.
754 1939.
756 Lincoln city centre.
757 River Bain.
758 Belton Wood.
759 Brigg just off the A15 and A18.
760 North Lincolnshire Museum, Scunthorpe.
761 Bourne.
762 G E Street RA.
763 1847.
764 Lincoln just off the A15.
765 Spilsby.
766 At Sandtoft, on part of the site of the former air base near Belton.
767 Sleaford.

768 1988.
769 Bourne on the A151.
770 The 1960s.
771 Spalding.
772 In the late 1920s.
773 The Humber Bridge and directly opposite North Ferriby.
774 King Charles I.
775 Skegness.
776 1686.
777 Plough Monday which marked the opening of the agricultural year.
778 Belton House.
779 King George III.
780 Grantham.
781 1939.
782 Barrow on Humber.
783 Scunthorpe.
784 1839.
785 Humberside.
786 £200 million.
787 John Hassall and was purchased by the railway company for the 12 guineas.
788 Saturdays.
789 1914.
790 Tuesday and Friday.
791 1948.
792 01754.
793 Viridius.
794 1851.
795 271 feet.
796 1851.
797 Grantham.
798 1869.
799 White Hart Hotel.
800 94.9 FM.

OTHER QUIZ BOOKS IN THIS SERIES:

THE DERBYSHIRE QUIZ BOOK
ISBN 978 1 906789 29 9 Paperback
Price: £7.99

THE GREAT YORKSHIRE QUIZ BOOK
ISBN 978 1 906789 34 3 Paperback
Price: £7.99

**THE GREAT NOTTINGHAMSHIRE
QUIZ BOOK**
ISBN 978 1 906789 42 8 Paperback
Price: £8.99